The official **BARMY** 🇬🇧 **ARMY**® book of cricket

BARMY
CRICKET

Published in 2006 by Barmy Army Productions (www.barmyarmy.com)

Designed by GPS Visual Communications,
Willow House, 47 West Street, Sutton, Surrey SM1 1SJ
020 8661 4100 (www.gpsvis.com)

Printed and bound in Italy by G.Canale & Co.

ISBN 0-9553754-0-1

ISBN 978-0-9553754-0-8

Many thanks to all the Barmy Army who sent in photography especially
Steve Power, Alex Cornwell, Charlie Britten and Alex Lowe.

Foreword

The Barmy Army is truly a phenomenon. They are that very rare thing, a group of like-minded individuals well-loved wherever they go. They spur the England team on through hard, energy-sapping days, they help keep the economies of any country they visit afloat. And they have the best interests of cricket at heart. Yes, their chanting can be tedious to some, yes, they drink too much and yes, they flout the safe sunbathing regulations. But they are a good thing. A very good thing. Just ask any of the England boys.

When we set up All Out Cricket magazine and put it on the newsstands in 2004, we did all those focus group things you are meant to do and found our target audience seemed to tally pretty much with the core membership of the Barmy Army. Cricket-lovers at heart, English patriots, love a laugh, want to get to know the players, keener on the social side of the game than the endless stats.

Th Barmy Army is often maligned by the more traditional cricket press, who tend to see them as moronic, boorish yobs, but they better watch out. The Barmy Army as an organisation is becoming a major force within the game. It is inclusive, plays a big part in the Cricket Foundation's Chance to Shine scheme and other charitable initiatives, organises colts cricket, and has an increasingly impressive advert-free website. It is a loose affiliation of people who represent the modern cricket fan – knowledgeable, nationalistic, affable, relatively wealthy, and bang up for a laugh. In essence it is a fan's union. The core support have been through the bad times with a smile on their faces – three drubbings in Australia spring to mind – and now the relatively good times are rolling, those smiles are broader than ever. And not for a minute do they moan about the Johnny-come-latelys who have only taken to cricket after England's Ashes successes. As far as they are concerned, the more the merrier.

It was on the 1994-'95 tour that the Barmy Army was born. Back then, the new breed of fan, chanting all day long, drinking all night long, happy all tour long, proved such an object of curiosity to the local press that they gave them a nickname. And it stuck. And how far they have come since then. All Out Cricket salutes the Army and is proud to have been able to help out in the production of this book, which encompasses what they are all about.

I was only too happy to help out when Paul Burnham, Barmy Army chief, asked me in desperation if I could find a ticket for Bill the Trumpeter to get into the ground to see a Test match. The occasion Monday 12 September 2005 at the Brit Oval, the last day of the Ashes Series. If one of the Army's icons hadn't been there, it wouldn't have been quite the same. That's the power of the union.

Matt Thacker
Editor, All Out Cricket

All Out Cricket editorial by Andy Afford, Matt Thacker, Phil Walker, Jim Hindson, Charmeyne McCollin and Dan Benson. All Out Cricket photography by Sam Bowles, Bowles Associates

HARMONY HISTORIES
THE ASHES TOUR 94/95

Songs. Where do they come from? Who first wrote On Ilkley Moor Ba Tat - and more to the point - why? Perhaps we'll never know. Perhaps we don't care. But somewhere - sometime - someone actually went to the trouble of writing it down, and thought - rightly or wrongly - that this is good stuff.

There's a whole shed load of songs like that. Songs with the words: "hey nonny nonny" in them, or "my love doth tarry" - generally sang by men with beards, or ill-looking women. The sort of songs you sometimes catch by accident as you scan up and down the dial looking for the Test Match on Long Wave, and instantly move on.

But the same applies to a whole bunch of half decent things that also fall under the "Traditional/ Anonymous" banner. Songs like "Frankie and Johnny" or "The House of the Rising Sun". Somebody wrote

them - but who, and why didn't they have a copyright lawyer?

Which leads us, neatly, to BARMY HARMONIES. Wouldn't it be a shame, and a missed opportunity, if one day people look up, say, "Everywhere we go" and see the words Otrad or Oanon after it. Again, you might say, what does it matter? Maybe you're right. But in BARMY CRICKET we have a unique chance to set the record straight - for once and for all.

So, with that in mind - we cornered Paul 'Leafy' Burnham, someone who was around when the whole thing kicked off, to try to nail down the facts.

And at the same time - through chatting about the songs - we might get a bit about the history of the Barmy Army without, hopefully, boring the four X out of everyone.

Now, as anyone who knows Paul will tell you, this is a bit like interviewing Oliver Reed about his acting roles - some of the recollections are probably as cloudy as the average Cricket Club pint of bitter, and for the same reasons.

But we gave it our best shot.....

Barmy Cricket (BC): Paul, the first tour, the first songs. What were they and who made them up?
Leafy: Well, it's a long story....

BC Keep it short then.
Leafy: It all started on the Ashes tour 94/95....

...the First Test Brisbane. The Aussies were being their usual witless selves. Throwing insults at the travelling fans and players, playing with their coloured beads, that kind of thing, when one English fan decided he'd had enough. He started to parade up and down in front of the Aussie section giving them a bit back. Not swearing but singing. I could see him from where I was but couldn't hear what he was on about. And the Aussies were throwing stuff at him, pouring beer over him, but he just kept on giving it back..

BC: And that was?
Leafy: Dave Peacock, soon to be known as Dave the General.

The good, the bad and the extremely ugly

BC: And the song?
Leafy: 'We came here with backpacks you with Ball and Chain'

BC: So that song originated in Brisbane?
Leafy: No.

BC: Could you enlarge on that answer?
Leafy: Well, obviously I wan't taking notes at the time, but I believe that song was first heard on the World Cup Tour two years earlier, maybe even as early as 1987? No one's really sure.

BC: So - going back to Brisbane - presumably Dave wasn't on his own for too long.
Leafy: No, by about day three a couple of guys in Forest shirts joined up with him as I recall, and by about day five there must have been about twenty or so - up and down in front of the Brisbane Hill. All the way they were doing an impression of convicts in a work gang walking slowly.

BC: And the Australians thought this was very funny of course.

Leafy: Most of them did actually; they were winning the cricket and had no problem with us showing some verbal retaliation to their brainless abuse.

BC: And how and when did the T-shirts and the identification of the Barmy Army come about?
Leafy: On the strength of the song, Dave Peacock ordered some T-Shirts with 'We came here with backpacks' on the front and 'You with Ball and Chain' on the back. This was one of the only Cricket related shirts available that you could buy on the tour. Personally I bought seven or eight of these shirts, basically because I didn't have time to wash the clothes I bought with me. Apart from this, the England fans wore their football shirts to distinguish themselves from the Aussies.

BC: Can you remember any Aussie songs?
Leafy: Yes. They had 3, all of which were sung in their traditional Australian Squeaky voices.. 1) "Look at the scoreboard" 2) Aussie Aussie Aussie, Oi Oi Oi 3) "Pommies Take it up the **** do dar, do dar"

BC: So they had 3 songs and were verbally abusing the English fans and players indiscriminately?
Leafy: The only one they didn't pick on was Darren Gough, who also soon became the first hero of the Barmy Army. The Aussies loved him.

BC: So, can you remember any of the other Barmy songs?
Leafy: I'll do my best.
  Imagine a one to one audience with Bruce Springsteen..... well, it was nothing like that. At this point, I began to realise why the Barmy Army sing in groups.... It is in the nature of communal songs that they tend to lose a bit without the raucous accompaniment . For example - have you ever seen the words of ,say, 'She Loves You' jotted down - they read like the rambling of your average Aussie. So - this is only to give the uninitiated a flavour of the proceedings but - even in transcription - you can see how constant repetition of phrases like 'We own your country', or 'You're just a part of our Empire', or 'You're just an English County' or 'Get your s**t stars off our flag', might get on the Aussies nerves after a while.

The entertainer 'Darren Gough'!

but originally Dave "The General" Peacock started it up in Brisbane having learnt it from 2 guys staying at his Backpackers.

(So - for those of you who haven't been to the cricket for a decade or so - this is how it goes. Its essentially a "call and response" number that even now never fails to get the most knackered of the Army up on their feet)

EVERYWHERE WE GO
Dave: Everywhere we go
Crowd: (Everywhere we go)
The people want to know
(The people want to know)
Who we are
(Who we are)
Where we come from
(Where we come from)
Shall we tell them
(Shall we tell them)
Who we are
(Who we are)
Where we come from
(Where we come from)
We are the Army
(We are the Army)
The Barmy Barmy Army
(The Barmy Barmy Army)
We are the England
(We are the England)
The Mighty Mighty England
(The Mighty Mighty England)
Atherton's Barmy Army
Etc.

So, these are some others that served a similar purpose:
'Captain Cook only stopped for a sh*t
Doo Dah, Doo DahSS.
We wish he hadn't bothered
Doo Dah Doo Dah Day'

'We're fat, we're round
3 dollars to the pound
Engerland, Engerland'

Away in a manger
No room for a bed
The little Lord Jesus
Lay down and he said
ENG–GER–LAND
ENG–GER–LAND
ENG–GER–LAND

'I can't read and I can't write
I must be Australian'

And - just to show that the Barmy Army aren't completely heartless - a couple for the Aussie kids:

'We're going to nick your sweets and lollipops'

'Back to school on Monday'.

Unsurprisingly, Phil Tufnell had his own personal favourite and always clapped his hands when he heard 'If you've all sh*gged an Aussie clap your hands'. And there was of course a bespoke Phil Tufnell tune:

'Philip Tufnell's having a party
Bring some drugs and a bottle of Bacardi'

BC: Aside from Tuffers, can you remember any of the other players numbers?
Leafy: Goughie, the Barmy idol, had his own personal number:

(to the tune of Lily the Pink)
'We'll Drink a drink a drink
To Goughie the King the King the King
He's the saviour of the England Team
He's the greatest cricketer that the world has ever seen'

BC: Wasn't the Barmy anthem "Everywhere We Go" originated on that tour?
Leafy: This has now become associated forever with Jimmy "you've only got one song" Flowers

BC: So, moving on from Brisbane. The next stop - Melbourne...
Leafy: We lost again. Shane Warne got a hat trick. It all seemed inevitable.

BC: What else?
Leafy: We learnt in the words of the song to 'always look on the bright side of life'. To ignore the arrogant Aussies and to make up more ditties and songs.

BC: What about Warnie?

Leafy: This man has had more songs written about him than any other Aussie or any other cricketer I suppose. Basically because he's so good, let's face it, and also he had such a great sense of humour in those days, and he still has. But the Aussie team were starting to respond to us. At one point we were all chanting "Stand Up if you hate Steve Waugh" and Warnie's reply was to get the whole of the slip cordon to sit down.

The supporters were also getting more and more arrogant at this point, so we started to sing "West Coast Eagles" songs. This was the Aussie Rules team who had recently beaten the Victorians! This wasn't received so well at times! The Victorians really do love their sport and hate to lose.

BC: So, two nil down. What happened in Sydney?

Leafy: Well, we were all able to get together on the famous Sydney Hill, which made a difference. As, of course, Gus Fraser did. So now the smaller groups who had been making up their own songs were now able to join together and the singing and chanting

A rare quiet moment for Dave trying to get cheap Milky Bars.

> "At one point we were all chanting 'Stand Up if you hate Steve Waugh' and Warnie's reply was to get the whole of the slip cordon to sit down."

Tuffers plus 'Deano' Headley

If only the skipper could say 'off with their heads'

IAN WOOLDRIDGE

GATTING decked

'Unfortunately, no,' said Graham. 'I would love to see them gassed but unfortunately that is not possible under Australian law.' This is a wholly politically incorrect remark and I support him. Our cricket may have been less than superlative on Monday but it was this small, banal bunch of louts in the crowd who really let our country down.

hours, is roughly an electric fire into your own das... Gatting had been in for 23 minutes. The ball billowed up into the angle between backward-square and short fine-leg, where

was relentless. England played well and Darren Gough made his famous fifty before lunch. Obviously the Barmy crowd loved every second of it.

Ironically, bad light saved Australia. The match was drawn. But a series that we had long since given up was resuscitated.

BC: So - in a sense was Sydney the beginning of the Barmy Army as we know it today?

Leafy: Definitely. The Australian media

had given up writing about how good they were and how poor we were on the cricket pitch and we became a sub-plot for the tour. We were christened "Barmy" for spending so much money following our team from one end of Australia to the other and "Army" because there were so many of us. Ian Wooldridge had written a negative article. We responded with an article in the Evening Standard at home stating "Ties or no ties" the Barmy Army love their cricket.

The British press merely looked down from their Ivory Tower and saw a load of football shirts and presumed we were all football fans. Which, of course, we were. Everyone supports football in England. But if we were football fans why would we all go away in the middle of the football season? We were, first and foremost, cricket fans. And ones that supported their team, win or lose, even though they were touring the other side of the world.

BC: Next up, Adelaide.

Leafy: We arrived in Adelaide and decided to produce shirts for the main group of boys who had been Christened the Barmy Army. They were T-Shirts and Polo Shirts with the Union Flag on the front and a map of Australia with all of the Test dates on it on the back. These shirts were immediately popular with not just the Barmy Army hard-core, but also other England fans. We historically won the

"Graham Thorpe grabbed centre stage at the Perth party, famously, Thorpie was last to leave the party singing his own song and walking into a glass door!"

test and the Barmy Army Merchandise Business, Brand Name and Supporters Club was formed almost over night.

BC: Do you think that the Barmy support made a difference?
Leafy: Well, obviously, I like to think so. It's impossible to say. But let's say that it is a happy coincidence that England's fortunes improved from Sydney onwards. By the time we arrived in Perth we couldn't retain the Ashes, but we could draw the series. After the victory in Adelaide the boys were singing "Go West to the WACA" which inspired a lot of Barmies to want to get over to Perth, the only problem being the distance; an appeal went out on South Australian Radio and some boys were able to get lifts from Aussies; other lads were even luckier and were able to get on a spare

carriage of the train that Sir Tim Rice was using for the journey. They sang all the way over to Perth, probably completely out of tune and to the horror of Tim Rice! The excitement was immense. Fair play to the Aussies though, the best team deservedly won the series. McDermot had a stormer and the Aussies Steam-rollered us, but the England team got a standing ovation from the Barmy Army.

BC: Did you get to speak with the players to see what they thought.
Leafy: We did get a chance to talk to the players, although Mumble would be a better description as by the time they arrived at our Barmy

Army parties in Adelaide and Perth most of us had been drinking all day. The Adelaide party was a celebration of the victory and most of the players turned up. We also organised an end of tour party at a nightclub in Perth.

Graham Thorpe grabbed centre stage at the Perth party, famously, Thorpie was last to leave the party singing his own song and walking into a glass door!

'There's only one Graham Thorpie
There's only one Graham Thorpie
Walking along, singing a song
Walking in a Thorpie wonderland'

That was the end of the Tour.......

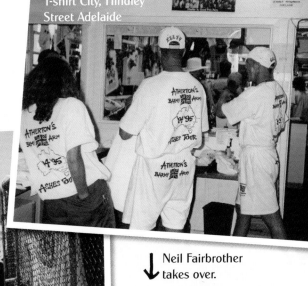

T-shirt City, Hindley Street Adelaide

Neil Fairbrother takes over.

The General and the boys on the march in Perth

MAN OF THE MOMENT:
Alastair Cook

At 21, on debut, Alastair Cook strolled into the history books. Welcome to the future, kids…you might want to shield your eyes.

It's funny how quickly things change. Two years ago Essex's Alastair Cook was just another teenager looking for a break. A brilliant colt, but still a kid hoping he could avoid the pitfalls, the crushed hopes and battered dreams, that befall so many other starlets in this, the cruellest of all games. Cricket, because it's played in the mind, destroys the merely gifted with a certainty not seen in any other sport. Talent, god-given, is so often left in the gutter.

Not so with Cook. Nothing is left on the cutting room floor with this boy. Welcome to a week in the life of an unusual 21-year-old…

Cook hotfoots it off the plane from Antigua, where he's been making hundreds for the 'A' team, and straight into a maelstrom. A handful of nets later, and with two of England's top six on planes home, he is told he's in for his debut. England win the toss, he straps them on. Rather like another callow 21-year-old English southpaw, his first scoring shot is an easy swivel-hook for four.

As others lose their heads, Cook sculpts the sort of innings expected of seasoned openers. He plays on for 60, his first overly ambitious shot in three hours of immaculately organised defence. It is fair to say he gets a bit tied down by Harbhajan; it is the first time he's faced him.

Two days later, he bats again. Three hours after taking guard, umpire Aleem Dar points out a banner in the crowd from an Indian girl asking for Cook's hand in marriage. Last week she didn't know who he was. Three hours after that, he's the youngest English centurion since that left-hander we mentioned earlier made three figures against Pakistan in 1978. That lad's name? David Gower.

There the similarities end. Gower was a dreamer, a free spirit, an impulse player who did impossible things, and whose ability to take us out of ourselves meant we forgave him those infuriating lost

> "He stepped up a grade straight away and that's due to his temperament."

This hundred by Cook is the 3000th century in Test cricket

UltraTech Cement

afternoons when he let us down. Cook, however, has few of the other's extravagances. He is, of course, Graham Gooch's protégé, so if Cook harboured any Gower-esque pretensions, you can be sure Goochie would send him off on another few laps around Chelmsford's outfield.

After Cook's cool 60, his mentor, who understands how to negotiate a new ball as well as any man in history, had this to say: "He stepped up a grade straight away and that's due to his temperament," said Gooch, speaking to the BBC. "The way he works at his game – he's very keen to learn. When you first come into international cricket you have to handle the cauldron of pressure. When you play county cricket the bowlers are of good quality but the pressure's not there. He played like I expected him to. He's got a lot of self-belief, he's very mature for his age, he's got a good temperament which will stand him in good stead for his career."

Cook was born to open. A compact technique built around a bat that comes down ramrod straight, he moves naturally inside the straight ball to whip it through the on-side, and generally eschews any cheek, occasionally allowing himself a punched cover-drive to keep the mind limber, but nothing more. Harbhajan tried to work him over, and although Cook rarely freed his arms, the instinctive way he recognised the doosra, rode the off-break, and manufactured runs on the leg-side suggested, no, *confirmed*, the emergence of a young player with the brain, nous and skill to score thousands.

England have unearthed another young kid who looks like he belongs in Test cricket's melting-pot. Composed, urbane, unflustered, clever – Ali Cook embodies the depth and quality of English cricket's new breed.

Now gather round, and let me tell you about Monty Panesar… ●

"He's got a lot of self-belief, he's very mature for his age, he's got a good temperament which will stand him in good stead for his career."

all out cricket

THE MAGAZINE THE PLAYERS READ

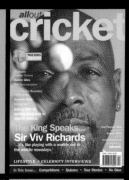

Subscribe at www.alloutcricket.co.uk

The Martin Peters
FACTOR

Remember Martin Peters? Footballer, got the ball down, sprayed it around? Scored the other goal in '66? Ahead of his time, they said. Should've been born 20 years later, when the game had caught up. But who is cricket's Martin Peters? England has Paul Collingwood – batter, bowler, fielder, top tourist, good temperament, a five-dimensional cricketer for the modern age. But who else?
Who else pre-empted cricket's changing moods? All Out Cricket's Phil Walker looks around.

Franklyn Stephenson
(first-class span 1981-1995)

The merry path trod by Franklyn Dacosta Stephenson took the smiling Bajan giant across the fields of Barbados, Gloucestershire, Notts, Orange Free State, Sussex, and Tasmania. Gangly, bearded and permanently amused by life's strange quirks, Stephenson oddly never played a Test match, but he was a towering figure on the county circuit throughout the eighties and nineties. As West Indies tore up the international order, a coterie of Caribbean understudies lit up the county game, from Sylvester Clarke to Wayne Daniel to Eldine Baptiste. They had charisma, class and, of course, serious wheels. Except with Franklyn, there was something else to his game besides extreme pace and devastating lower-order hitting (12 first-class hundreds, huge leverage). Of his 792 first-class and 448 one-day wickets, a good few hundred must have been pilfered by his legendary slower-ball.

Bounding in from his immense height, a batsman would be anchored on the back-foot anticipating another fizzer past the face. Often, that was exactly what he got. But just when he felt an iota of comfort – duck, duck, weave, missed hook, duck – Stephenson dropped in a slower ball that would make the batsman recoil from the expected beamer, leaving him looking at the 'keeper as the ball thudded either onto his toe or the base of the stumps. Nowadays we see exponents play around with the skill all the time, especially in one-dayers, although there are numerous examples when it's paid off in Test cricket – Courtney Walsh to Graham Thorpe, lbw as Thorpe turned away expecting the 90mph beamer; Chris Cairns famously nutmegging Chris Read as he ducked for cover; Stephen Harmison mugging Michael Clarke last summer.

Yet back in Stephenson's day, batsmen were unaccustomed to such cheek, and Franklyn's particular beauty soon became the talk of many an edgy dressing room. In time, others would start to experiment...

Geoff Humpage
(1974-1990)

It's generally accepted that Gilchrist's arcing blade caused teams to stop searching for the perfect wicket-keeping technician, and look instead for a competent gloveman who doubled up as a destructive middle-order batsman. Maybe, on the world stage. But talk to wizened Warwickshire loyalists of a certain vintage, and they will brusquely direct you to the majestically named Geoff Humpage as proof that the craze started way before some Aussie gunslinger barged into town and claimed the honour for himself.

Humpage, as chunky and broad as the name suggests, was a star at Edgbaston. The members loved him – there was a touch of the village green meshed around his undoubted class – and for 16 years he heartily guarded the timbers and whacked away from the middle-order. A final first-class average of 36 and over 18,000 runs, with 29 hundreds and a top score of 254, bore testament to his then unique qualities as English cricket's first genuine batsman-'keeper. During the late seventies and early eighties England had two great craftsmen in Bob Taylor and Alan Knott, so the prevailing philosophy of the time meant Humpage never made a Test team. He did, however, play three ODIs against Australia in 1981, with limited success. In another era he'd have played 100.

Douglas Jardine
(1920-1933)

Most cricket fans know of Douglas Jardine, but not for his modest record of one century in just 22 Tests. They know about him for one reason, one series, one moment in cricket history when the ruthless professionalism of the future collided with the Corinthian ethic of its past. As every schoolboy knows, Jardine was the man behind 'Bodyline' and in his hands cricket was changed forever. And whatever the morality of the aristocrat's decision to instruct working-class miner Harold Larwood to aim for the heads of Australian batsmen to stop runs and invoke fear, the tactic was revolutionary, and enduring. Watch Brett Lee for ten minutes if you're still unsure.

The reason was Bradman. Because the boy was too good, Jardine devised a plan to stop him. He figured if he packed the leg-side and got his quickest bowler to bowl at his head, even a genius could be clipped. And it worked. Bradman's average was halved, and England duly won the series 4-1. To Jardine, the hospitalisation of Aussie wicket-keeper Bert Oldfield after a deadening thunk to the temple was merely an unfortunate by-product.

Unwittingly perhaps, Jardine ushered in the modern game. Maybe it just stemmed from a pathological desire to be the 'winner', to outdo in the mind those blessed with greater natural ability. Maybe he knew fair means would return him to England a broken captain. Maybe he just hat-

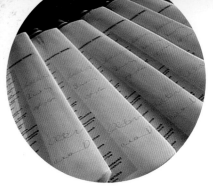

ed Aussies as much as popular myth suggests. Whatever the reasons, from that series tea and scones and half-volleys to get you started were out; in came hustle, bite, sledging and batteries of quicks.

This was the modern game as you see it now, 1932-33 vintage.

Colin Bland
(1956-1973)

Fielding is the one area where cricket has irrefutably improved. Players are fitter now, more athletic, and the prevalence of limited-over knock-abouts mean a top fielder saves 30 runs before he straps the pads on. In the age of ultra-professionalism, it's not unusual to see baseball coaches bark orders across international outfields before play starts, honing throwing techniques.

Back in the sixties, South Africa's Colin Bland must have seen the future. A decent batsman without ever suggesting greatness, Bland featured in 21 Tests and made a few runs, but his place in cricket's story was assured through the brilliance of his out-fielding. On SA's tour of England in 1966, whenever he was willing, crowds would flock to the outfield during lunch breaks to be astonished by Bland fielding exhibitions. His speed to the ball, natural athleticism and flexibility (uncommon among great cover fielders, Bland was a tall man) made him one of the draws of the summer, and his famous run-outs of Barrington and Parks at Lord's turned the match in SA's favour.

His arm was his greatest strength.

At a time when fielding was not valued, Bland would practise throwing at one stump until he was confident of hitting every other time he took aim. These days, it's all part of the cricketer's daily routine. Back then, Bland prowled the covers alone.

Mark Taylor
(1985/86-1998/99)

In 1993, when the affable, genial Mark 'Tubby' Taylor took over from Allan Border as Australian captain, many felt the hard, abrasive edge Border had instilled would be lost. Not a bit of it.

Taylor took his predecessor's principle of never knowing you're beaten, shook it about a bit, and constructed a results-machine that forgot how to lose. But what Taylor also managed, and what must be his greatest achievement, was to make this Australian team forget how to draw too.

He reasoned that with the advent of one-day cricket, players were playing more shots with a more attacking mindset. Batsmen were hitting balls they would have left alone in another era, and bowlers were constantly trying something different to get a wicket. Attritional cricket suddenly seemed outmoded, and Taylor was the first to seize on this. He proposed that his team actively look to score at four runs per over, bringing at least 360 runs per day. Over five days, he concluded, only the flattest pitch could preclude a positive result.

Taylor backed his players to maintain that scoring rate. He made his dislike of drawn Test matches public, stating he wanted to eradicate it from his side altogether. It was a maxim seamlessly taken on by Steve Waugh when he was handed the captaincy, and armed with a more complete team at its peak, he oversaw Australia's famous run of 16 straight Test wins.

Waugh may have taken the credit

but it was Taylor who put the wheels in motion, and this unsafety-first philosophy has since spread: in 2004 England won seven Tests from seven, and outpacing Australia's batsmen last summer. India and Pakistan spent their last series smacking a boundary every six balls. This is the modern way, it's great to watch, and Taylor is the visionary who made it possible.

England player Q&A's

PAUL COLLINGWOOD

BEST UMPIRE:

Under pressure	Steve Bucknor
Personality Manner with players	Venkat
	Neil Mallender
Hat	Dickie Bird
Mannerisms	Billy Bowden

BEST BATSMAN:

Temperament	Jacques Kallis
Ability/talent Best looker	Brian Lara Michael Vaughan
Fitness	Herschelle Gibbs
Concentration Bravery	Jacques Kallis Matthew Hoggard

BEST FIELDER:

Throw	Andrew Flintoff
Hands	Andrew Flintoff
Speed	Herschelle Gibbs
Athleticism	Andrew Symonds
Bravery	Andrew Strauss

FANTASY SLIP CORDON

ALL OUT CRICKET'S IAN SYKES HAS A DREAM...

WICKET-KEEPER – Jimmy Saville
Don't get me wrong, I think he's a bit of an idiot. But I look back fondly to the days when any keeper worth his salt had to be mad as a badger. Saville is as mad as a whole set, and I like that in a man. He might even be able to smoke out the top order with a fat Cuban.

FIRST SLIP – Robbie Fowler
Praise be to Bob. Every time we took a wicket, we could do that celebration where we impersonate a cow eating grass, or something. And he might even give me a house.

SECOND SLIP – Me
Good hands, epic concentration and a keen eye for necessary field changes. I'm in like Flynn.

THIRD SLIP – My dad
Although he was reputedly the best cover fielder in the Merseyside Competition during the 1970s, I reckon he'd much rather have a stint in the slips these days. A good opportunity for father and son to spend the afternoon chewing the fat and slagging off the opening bat's 'dominant bottom hand' as he thumps his way to a ton.

FOURTH SLIP – Hermann Maier
Since his first World Cup victory in 1997, 'The Herminator' has been well known for his fearless approach to downhill skiing. After nearly breaking his back in a dramatic fall at the 1998 Winter Olympics, he dusted himself down and got back on his skis to take the gold medal just days later. In 2001, Maier was almost killed in a motorcycle accident and narrowly avoided having his leg amputated. After massive reconstructive surgery, the consensus was that his career was over. Just two weeks after his return to competition in January 2003, he won the super-G victory in his native Austria. In 2003-2004, his first full season back, he won the super-G World Cup and the overall competition for the fourth time in his career, a feat widely seen as one of the greatest comebacks in sports history. 'The Herminator' is a credit to mankind, and can be my fourth slip any time.

GULLY – A chimpanzee – ever since I was a kid I wanted my own chimp, but my mum never let me have one. Even today, my wife isn't keen. It might be a bit of an indulgence on my part, but it's my fantasy slip cordon, so at gully, I'd like a chimp. Preferably one that didn't eat his own poo.

SECOND GULLY – Terry Nutkins – digitally challenged otter botherer Nutkins might not be catch-tastic, but he does have other qualities. As much as I love chimps, we need Tel on hand for when the shit goes down. I've seen Chimp Week on BBC1 and the little bastards can get out of hand.

BARMY COMMENT:
Fair Play

Out Man In The Stands takes an impartial Barmy Army look at the Ins and Not Outs of FAIR PLAY whilst also managing to have a pop at your favourite and mine, Shane Warne. Again...

Imagine this scenario. A Test match. England against Australia, say. Shane Warne bowling. A suspicion of an inside edge on to pad. None of the Aussie fielders go up.

Ponting turns quietly to Warney.

"Do you think he touched it, mate?"

"Can't be sure. Let's play on, what do you think?"

"Yeah, bad luck, mate."

And then Strauss, say, turns to Ponting.

"Actually, old thing, I think I got a nick. I'm off."

Yes, I know, ridiculous. If you were pitching that as a film idea you'd have to have to call it Fantasy. Science Fiction. Right next to your 'When Freddie Kruger Met Sally', or 'Harry Potter and the Boring Maths Lesson'.

Noone's going to buy it.

Okay. Two points here. No one's going to 'walk' at the moment when no one else does, and there is a chance that actually you'd feel you were letting down your team-mates.

How to resolve this? First thing. We have TV technology. Isn't it a ridiculous thing when the only two people in a packed Test Arena who don't know when someone is out or not are the two old guys in white coats in the middle (and also my mate Andy T - but he's just a bit slow!)

Now - hopefully - this discussion will soon be dated as they'll do the sensible thing and take advantage of the technology. They say it will hold the game up? Are you kidding! Have

you seen the over rate these days? A better idea would be Cheer Leaders to keep us amused in the time it takes for the bowler to get back to his mark.

Also. this would hopefully reduce the situation where a fielder maybe catches the ball off an inside edge and runs towards the Umpire, face contorted, like a combination of a Maori Haka and someone who has just won a Rolls Royce in some crappy Saturday night Gameshow.

Personally, I would create a ruling whereby only the bowler is allowed to appeal. You can celebrate the catch (I think that without physically putting the players in straightjackets they will always do that!) but not

As his chair collapsed from under him, Leafy regretted having that last pie ...

> "I mean, Shane Warne, summer, 2005? Was there a delivery where he didn't appeal, or look puzzled, or hard done by. Did he appeal when Freddie smacked him for six on one of those many occasions? I think he probably did."

actually appeal. I don't know - maybe I'm old fashioned.

I think that in too many sports they are reluctant to change the rules - even when it's obvious. In football, am I the only person who hates the fact that players are seen to mouth off to the linesmen and the ref - obviously f-ing this that and the other - and nothing happens! If you spoke to someone like that in the street you'd get a clip round the ear, or worse, so why is it acceptable in Sport?

Also the way in which the players are allowed to get in each others shirts at Set Piece play and you never see a free kick given - certainly never a penalty.

Ah well, that's football....

Which brings me back to cricket and appealing. Appalling appealing. Do the players practise it in front of the mirror?

Will there soon be a TV Talent Contest on Saturday Nights - Peak Time viewing (where all the absolutely crap programmes live!) "Not Out!" - where players have to appeal in front of a panel of Simon Callow and Dickie Bird and Mark Nicholas and they

have to judge whether they would have given it or not?

"Personally, I wasn't convinced. What about you, Dickie?"

"Me neither Simon lad..."

I mean, Shane Warne, summer, 2005? Was there a delivery where he didn't appeal, or look puzzled, or hard done by. Did he appeal when Freddie smacked him for six on one of those many occasions? I think he probably did.

I wonder if he's like that in every day life. When he used to

ask out women, and they turned him down... Would he stand there, look up to the heavens, rub his chin with his hands, then laugh to himself and shake his head, before walking slowly back to the bar. I think he probably did.

Maybe, people like all that stuff. Maybe it adds to the Theatre of it. For me, it's dissent. The implication is that the umpire is a dribbling fool who doesn't know his Out from his elbow.

If you want Theatrical behaviour go to the Circus! (says he, "Mr Angry!")

So - let's hear it for TV Technology - for less dissent - and more Fair Play!

I have to finish now to go stop those flying pigs crapping all over my garden.

YOUR MAN IN THE STANDS

Excuse me Freddie this young lady was definitely first at the bar!

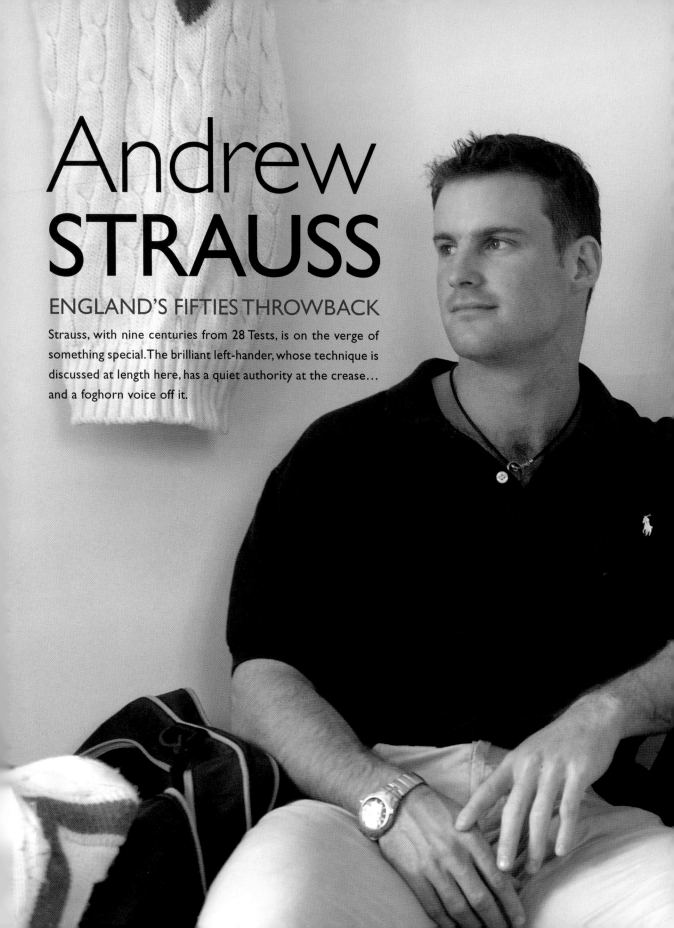

Andrew STRAUSS

ENGLAND'S FIFTIES THROWBACK

Strauss, with nine centuries from 28 Tests, is on the verge of something special. The brilliant left-hander, whose technique is discussed at length here, has a quiet authority at the crease… and a foghorn voice off it.

Louder than bombs is Andrew Strauss. Louder than effin' bombs. So deafening in fact that a mere ten seconds of him talking into his mobile handset has stopped all conversation and activity in one of England's team room at Loughborough. Stopped it stone dead. The timbre of the voice is full baritone, the clarity and enunciation that of a media-trained Tory back bencher, the volume all West End *'can you hear me at the back'* theatrical. Boom, boom… boom.

Strauss, oblivious to the impact he is having, faces out of the computer suite window at the National Cricket Centre. He's talking definitively to an inquiring journalist about England's prospects in India. And in exactly the time it takes for him to bellow 'Hi, Andy Strauss here,' into the receiver he has brought the curtain down on any chatter in the room, replacing it with knowing shakes of the head, resigned half smirks and the subsequent swing of closing doors.

A pre-prescribed ten minutes later and he is off his phone. He greets us with a firm grip, unwavering eye contact and another glass-shattering 'Hi, Andy Strauss.'

He is a new dad. As was widely reported, Australian actress wife Ruth gave birth to a son, Samuel David recently, with Strauss returning home on paternity leave from England's 2005-06 tour of Pakistan. Against the protocol of the past maybe, but as stated at the time by the Middlesex left-hander, some things in life are more important than cricket. An enlightened outlook for arguably one of England's more old-fashioned cricketers.

Born in Johannesburg, South Africa in 1977, Strauss, prior to England selection, had proven himself a consistent turn in domestic cricket before forcing his way initially into the one-day side on the 2003 tour to Sri Lanka. A début Test hundred at Lord's against New Zealand in 2004 established his international pedigree and hastened Nasser Hussain into retirement. And he has rarely looked back since. Nine hundreds in 28 Tests have seen comparisons made with the very best of England openers. Strauss appears here to stay.

His left-handed style and manner is undoubtedly old school. Educated at Radley College and Durham University, where he secured a BA in Economics, there is nothing new-fangled about Strauss. His persona, tempo of innings, and deftness of stroke are the stuff

Photo: All Out Cricket

of cricket scenes that have been re-enacted across the playing fields of England for generations.

He is always fluent with the bat. And whilst batting, he is happy to catch the eye of a bowler, acknowledge a good delivery and even laugh at himself and his predicament should things go haywire, something that is in short supply at the high-achieving end of professional sport. Witness the occasion when he scored the first of two Ashes hundreds last season. He completed his second innings 106 at Old Trafford with a lump of sticking plaster attached to his left ear, having been hit by a searing Brett Lee bouncer. Asked about it, he said that it was fine but: "It's not doing much for my street cred."

According to teammates, credibility has never been an issue for Strauss – his absolute lack of fashion sense has NEVER been questioned. He is

Photo: All Out Cricket

consistently the player voted the least trendy member of the squad. And on our meeting, despite him having all the obligatory elements of the Team England informal off-duty uniform – padded life-preserver jacket, designer jeans, Timberland boots and beanie hat – it somehow doesn't quite come home to roost on Strauss. Pietersen carries it off. Vaughan the same. Even Hoggard. But not 'Lord Brocket', as he is occasionally referred to by colleagues. And that's a good thing.

Since entering Test cricket, his batting has surreptitiously changed. Looking at earlier videotape as preparation for this interview (Strauss has been doing the same of late), his footwork in defence has evolved. In those early days he was more inclined to defend off the front foot. Deliveries pitching around the grey edges of a good length, in the past were consistently and resolutely met with the high part of the bat, Strauss pushing forward. But things have changed. These are now

> "I'm not certain, but I do think that the ability to adapt is the key to success in Test cricket. You've always got to look to evolve and keep on top of your technique."

more regularly negotiated with the lower middle of the bat playing back. It is a modification that has pluses and minuses attached.

Strauss, in his strokeplay as a back foot player, has most excited the pundits. Michael Atherton described the opener's cut stroke as the best he's ever seen. And his hooking, pulling and hitting square of the wicket have all become signature strokes. But is he now consciously looking for these shots more than before? Where in the past they would happen more organically, could he be accused of forcing things? I broached the question; is he mindful of hanging back and looking for the short ball more: "Yeah, definitely," he says, sitting comfortably with the technical appraisal. "I think you're exactly right. I do hang back more. I played a lot of cricket before being picked for England. As a county opener you generally get to face a lot of seamers operating at around 78-80mph, who look to pitch the ball up. Because of that, you're more likely to score off fuller balls and you look for these as bowlers try to swing the ball at you. In Test cricket you've got guys bowling at 88-90mph and if anything they're going to drop a bit short. That's where your scoring margins are likely to be.

"I'd say that although my game has changed a lot, I do think that I still look to do the fundamentals the same. You still have to be able to keep the good balls out. And if I get that right, I

give myself the best chance possible to make runs."

After a début year of unprecedented success, peaking with the scoring of 656 runs on England's victorious trip to South Africa, touring Pakistan coincided with the only form blip of Strauss' international career. A hundred in India silenced the doubters, but it was a tough baptism in Pakistan, a fact borne out by Strauss himself: "I did struggle to adapt, I think we all did (Strauss made scores of 9, 23, 12 and 0). We played on a couple of dodgy pitches in the warm-up games and no one went into the Tests having spent any time in the middle. Batting against the new ball was different to anywhere else I'd played and possibly a bit of a glimpse into how it will be in India. The ball skids lower with the new ball than it does with the older one. I just didn't get to grips with it."

When asked why that was the case, Strauss replied: "I'm not certain, but I do think that the ability to adapt is the key to success in Test cricket. You've always got to look to evolve and keep on top of your technique. Bad habits

SPEAKY'S CORNER

can creep in and it's very important that you develop new shots to stop bowlers getting used to bowling to you. Duncan Fletcher is particularly good at that, prodding us into mentally looking at match situations with fresh eyes, giving us more clarity about our game and an extra focus.

"As for playing last winter, maybe I learnt that it's a lot easier to hook a ball bowled at 80mph than it is at 90mph! Also, early on in your innings the cut and pull shots aren't perhaps such valuable

shots to you out in India and Pakistan. It's all about learning and adapting."

Strauss, in his critical appraisal of his own game and his striving for an ever-evolving repertoire of scoring options and knowledge, highlights most dramatically the mindset of the modern international player. He is looking for any advantage he can gain to place himself in a position to score more runs off what can be argued are only moderately loose deliveries. His gameplan, like England as a whole, is built around attack.

Considering whether Strauss' de-camping increasingly to the back foot is good, bad or neither, needs some background. Unquestionably, batting when pared back to the very basics, becomes more precarious when the ball is directed at the wicket. Although the threat of serious injury is significantly lessened, up goes the likelihood of getting out. When a ball is pitched up to hit the stumps, every manner of dismissal is in play. When the ball is short of a good length, bowlers are pinning all their hopes on a catch.

Because of these percentages, master technician Geoffrey Boycott constantly re-affirms the need to play forward if at all possible, in order to negate swing movement, seam movement, shooters, lifters and the wrath of the

"I think it's best to go out there fresh. Better than going out to bat with the side 20-2 and knowing that Shoaib Akhtar is bowling at 95mph"

commentator himself. Boycott's is a philosophy born out of a 'playing the percentages' technique and a defence-first mindset. Strauss, although he may look a bit of a throwback, even resembling technicians of Sir Geoff's era in his demeanour and manner on the field, rather obviously isn't.

With the interview over, we set about tackling photographs. A temporary studio has been readied, but a prop is needed. Strauss is asked to supply his bat. And, as he heads for the door to fetch it he asks over his shoulder if he needs to change? Although an initial request for him to strip to the waist and oil himself up is knocked back with a wry 'not in the state I'm in' and references to a post-Christmas six-week lay-off, I do

wonder about the question's other meaning. Does he need to change, as a player?

There is a freshness about his game that makes you smile. He appears to play with utter freedom, although he admits to suffering with nerves on occasions and says he just masks them well. His joy at taking a catch is infectious and although he admits to having found it tough, to the point of being 'unfair', as a left-hander facing Shane Warne, he wouldn't have it any other way.

To end things, I state that he would of course like to slide down the batting order to the calmer waters of the middle order. Strauss shoots me a look: "For what reason [Laughs]… What are you trying to say? [Laughing even more]". I state that I thought

all openers fancied entering the fray when the shine has been knocked off the new ball by some other poor sap? "No I don't think so," he says, "I think it's best to go out there fresh. Better than going out to bat with the side 20-2 and knowing that Shoaib Akhtar is bowling at 95mph and hitting everyone. Sometimes it's just best to get out there, unaware what's happening."

So does he need to change? With an attitude of going out there with a fresh mind, working hard at his game, seeming fearless and playing with freedom even though he doesn't feel that way, well, I think he'll be OK for a bit. ●

THE OUTTAKES
Strauss On…

Why his son was only given two initials, rather than the anticipated 'always going to play for England' three: "We didn't think that we'd go down the full jazz hat route. We kept it nice and simple, his name's Sam."

The likelihood of falling under the long lens of the paparazzi when shopping in Sainsburys: "Not really. I think that's more Kevin Pietersen than Andrew Strauss. I've definitely been recognised more since last year, people coming up and saying how much they enjoyed the Ashes. I think that I get the good side of the attention rather than the intrusion."

What he would most like to change about his batting? Strauss goes for the kitchen sink approach: "I'd like to bat like Brian Lara."

On his voice: "I'm told it's loud, but for some reason I just can't hear it."

Taken from All Out Cricket magazine, available from WHSmith or subscribe at www.alloutcricket.co.uk

PACE TO BURN

Are England the new West Indies? Michael Vaughan's 2005 Ashes quartet have to be the fastest collective on the planet and BA looks at the challenge of facing them. And we ask Michael Holding to let us know if there are any similarities between this four and the Windies' battery of quick men of the Eighties.

It is day two of the first Ashes Test at Lord's and Australia are on top in the match, but, let's remember before we start consigning England to the scrapheap, have had it far from easy. Langer has been hit on the elbow, Hayden on the helmet, Ricky Ponting in the face; all in the first hour of the match. The Aussie tail has been targeted mercilessly and over the course of the match three of the four England seamers have operated at higher than 90mph – and not for just the odd ball.

According to the radar gun, Glamorgan's Simon Jones has bowled a ball at 96mph. With every three mph, at the top end of the speed register, roughly equivalent to a yard of pace, the Welshman bowled at times, two whole yards quicker than Brett Lee's average of 90mph, outstripping all but Worcestershire's current overseas Shoaib Akhtar in terms of sheer velocity.

In the late seventies and throughout the eighties, fast bowling used to be the sole preserve of the all-powerful and all-conquering West Indies. Marshall, Daniel, Garner, Roberts,

SWOT Analysis

Hoggard, Jones, Flintoff and Harmison – the best England attack for 20 years! But what do they offer, individually? BA runs the rule over the quartet in this insightful SWOT analysis.

HARMISON

FULL NAME: Stephen James Harmison
BORN: October 23, 1978, Ashington, Northumberland
AGE: 27
HEIGHT: 6'6"
COUNTY: Durham
ROLE: Right-handed batsman, right-arm fast bowler
ENGLAND DEBUT: India at Trent Bridge, 2002
CAPS: 31
FIVE WICKET HAULS: 6
TEST WICKETS: 129
BEST BOWLING: 7-12 v West Indies at Jamaica, 2003/04
QUICKEST BALL: 95.6mph
OPERATING SPEED: 85-91mph

DELIVERIES BOWLED: Stephen Harmison's stock ball is a rising delivery that hits high on the bat on a line on or around the top of off stump. He has the ability to swing the new ball away from the right-handed batsman and bowls an awkward short ball at the ribs. When confident, can also produce a devastating yorker.

STRENGTHS: Harmison has the longest levers in the game, making him able to deliver the ball from 'multi-storey' height. Not only does he generate steep bounce, but also searing pace. When these are combined, Harmison is the toughest physical challenge in cricket.

WEAKNESSES: Can prove susceptible to dips in confidence that seems largely linked with being away from home. Harmison is a well-known sufferer from homesickness.

OPPORTUNITIES: For all the pace he generates, he is slight of build. As he gets physically stronger, additional upper body power will translate into the ability to maintain consistent repetition of his action, something that has on occasions let him down.

THREATS: Over-bowling Harmison must be a worry and with bowling fast comes the chance of injuries and time on the sidelines. Harmison has had back problems in the past, missing England's tour to Sri Lanka in 2003/04. He will need skilful handling to help prolong his career over the next seven or eight years.

THE VERDICT: Anyone who finds themselves ranked number one in the world, in anything, has to have something about them. Facing Harmison takes courage. On his day and on his game, the Ashington Express is the perfect mix of youthful endeavour, just enough experience and natural talent. Harmison has the potential to be England's all-time leading wicket-taker.

Croft, Patterson, Moseley, Walsh, Clarke, Ambrose to name but a few. All individually very dangerous, but as a collective – unstoppable.

Possibly the most evocative of all the names is Michael Holding. The ever-lean Jamaican raised the mechanics of whizzing a five and a half ounce piece of leather around a batsman's ears to the level of art. With his trademark relaxed saunter to the wicket, for all the world like a world-class 400 metre runner, all 'Mikey' was short of was a bend and a baton.

Holding, and the West Indies, ➤

FLINTOFF

FULL NAME: Andrew Flintoff
BORN: December 6, 1977, Preston, Lancashire
AGE: 28
HEIGHT: 6'4"
COUNTY: Lancashire
ROLE: Right-handed batsman, right-arm fast bowler
ENGLAND DEBUT: South Africa at Trent Bridge, 1998
CAPS: 48
FIVE WICKET HAULS: 1
TEST WICKETS: 123
BEST BOWLING: 5-58 v West Indies at Bridgetown, 2003/04
QUICKEST BALL: 94mph
OPERATING SPEED: 86-90mph
DELIVERIES BOWLED: Heavy ball after heavy ball. Back of a length, angled in at the right-hander, ball after ball after ball. England's enforcer, merciless in his dishing out of 'the short and nasty'.

STRENGTHS: A model of consistency and possessing the heart of a lion with ball in hand, Flintoff's second and third spells when all seems lost have turned many a day back in his team's favour.
The desire to turn 200-3 and all against England, to 240-5 and back in the balance makes him indispensable to Michael Vaughan. Bowls brilliantly to left-handers, having the ability to get the ball to go away from them from both over and around the wicket. Leathers the ball into the wicket when bowling at the tail. No easy runs or respite.

WEAKNESS: At times lacks that knocked-down unplayable jaffa. Can get into a plodding mode and can overdo the short stuff.

OPPORTUNITIES: A genuinely world-class performer with bat, ball or in the slip cordon. Flintoff is still a relatively inexperienced bowler, coming into his own in the last two years after his early career was blighted by injury. The more he learns his craft, the better he will become.

THREATS: Bowling looks hard work for Flintoff. There is nothing easy on the eye about the action and the ball is forced down the other end by brute strength and will power. This has to prove taxing on the body and Flintoff runs the risk of finding himself 'up on bricks' from time to time and occasionally in need of a re-fit or re-furb.

THE VERDICT: A legend in the making. Just needs to rack up multiple series wins over Australia… piece of cake.

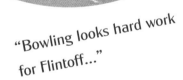

"Bowling looks hard work for Flintoff…"

pioneered a style of bowling (the bodyline series in 1932/33 aside) that was the most psychologically and physically intimidating ever seen, preying on the batsman's mind as much as their technique. As they say, some people drink to remember, others to forget and over five and six-Test series, if England's tail-enders weren't quite diving for the scotch bottles of an evening, they were certainly contemplating it.

As the West Indies pre-eminence as cricket's top dog waned, so did

JONES

NAME: Simon Philip Jones
BORN: December 25, 1978, Morriston, Swansea, Glamorgan, Wales
AGE: 27
HEIGHT: 6'3"
COUNTY: Glamorgan
ROLE: Left-handed batsman, right-arm fast bowler
ENGLAND DEBUT: India at Lord's, 2002
CAPS: 15
TEST WICKETS: 44
FIVE WICKET HAULS: 1
BEST BOWLING: 5-57 v West Indies at Port of Spain, 2003/04
QUICKEST BALL: 96mph
OPERATING SPEED: 85-88mph
DELIVERIES BOWLED: Attacks the stumps and is England's best reverse-swinger of the ball. In recent times has developed a good away-swinger to the right-hander.

STRENGTHS: Generates skiddy bounce and is very deceptive, pace-wise. Has proven increasingly reliable for his captain and can bowl long penetrative spells with the old ball. Can bowl startling snorters out of nowhere that undo the best.

WEAKNESSES: Too many four balls. Jones pitches the ball up and if he doesn't control his lengths perfectly, can concede runs down the ground. Giving up driven boundaries can render him under-used by Vaughan, placing the burden of an increased workload on the other three quick men. Has been England's fourth seamer over the last year, some way behind the other three.

OPPORTUNITIES: Jones seems to be developing nicely after over a year out following knee surgery. Has looked one-dimensional in the past, most effective when the ball is old and reversing. But an improved wrist position at point of release has made Jones a difficult customer whenever he bowls.

THREATS: If Jones doesn't bowl the amount of overs that his captain needs, the tall and more angular Chris Tremlett waits in the wings. For Jones to stay in the side he needs to bowl. If he bowls a lot, he could prove a match-winner.

THE VERDICT: Increased versatility as a bowler now makes Simon Jones a genuine wicket-taking threat. The ability to bowl quickly and maintain a full length makes him a bowler that should also fare well overseas.

"You'd have to say that, yes; England's bowlers do all have a reasonable amount of pace. Without that you can't be aggressive. Even Matthew Hoggard, the slowest of the four, isn't slow."

their kennel of bowlers. Replaced by Pakistan's Imran Khan, Wasim Akram and Waqar Younis as the world's most evocative names, with their own way of doing things.

Theirs was a vastly different science. It was still built on pace, but was honed on the slow and unresponsive wickets of the sub-continent, and relied on swing. With no bounce and seam movement to exploit, these resourceful cricketers were able to work with the dynamics and deteriorating properties of the ball and make it bend round corners. Where the great Windies attacks hammered away at the batsman, bowling short of a length with a packed slip cordon and everyone else square of the wicket or behind, Wasim and Waqar did it themselves. Tailing the ball back into the wickets from outside off stump, for them the fielders (wicket-keeper aside) were nigh on obsolete.

But here we are again, 30 years on and the chin music is again playing across Lord's. And what does Holding make of it all: "You'd have to say that, yes; England's bowlers do all have a reasonable amount of pace. Without that you can't be aggressive. Even Matthew Hoggard, the slowest of the four, isn't slow."

Holding was reluctant to draw comparisons between then and now. But he did agree that there was a similarity in approach, if not style: "Flintoff and Harmison are possibly the most like West Indies quick bowlers. They are the tallest and most aggressive. They are certainly well capable of bouncing the ball ➤

HOGGARD

FULL NAME: Matthew James Hoggard
BORN: December 31, 1976, Leeds, Yorkshire
AGE: 29
HEIGHT: 6'3"
COUNTY: Yorkshire
ROLE: Right-handed batsman, right-arm fast-medium bowler
ENGLAND DEBUT: West Indies at Lord's, 2000
CAPS: 41
FIVE WICKET HAULS: 5
TEST WICKETS: 160
BEST BOWLING: 7-61 v South Africa at Johannesburg, 2004/05
QUICKEST BALL: 88mph
OPERATING SPEED: 79-84mph
DELIVERIES BOWLED: Hoggard is an away-swing bowler in the classic English tradition. Also runs the ball away from the left-hander, rather than actually swinging it. Bowls a good bouncer that can draw instinctive and ill-advised hooks from napping batsmen.

STRENGTHS: Persistence personified. Hoggard keeps on running in and is of immense value to his side. The slowest of the England attack, but arguably the most skillful, Matthew Hoggard rarely lets you down.

WEAKNESSES: Faced with a flat pitch and a ball that refuses to swing, Hoggard can look pedestrian.

OPPORTUNITIES: Hoggard is vital to England's hopes. If he bowls a high volume of overs it allows the three out-and-out quickies to bowl in short sharp bursts. If Hoggard could find an extra yard of pace it would allow him to maintain a slightly shorter length and not run the risk of being pulled on docile wickets.

THREATS: Because he's a workhorse and not a thoroughbred, any dip in form is noticed. When tired Hoggard's action can look slingy, making him prone to leak balls down the leg side.

THE VERDICT: Hoggard is another England bowler that brings something different to the party. Tireless in attitude and forthright of manner, Hoggard is Yorkshire through and through. A great bloke and the England bowler closest to reaching 200 Test wickets.

and forcing the batsmen onto the back foot."

When asked of all the pacemen he operated with, which quartet he felt to be the best, the answer came easy: "For me it has to be the original four of Andy Roberts, Colin Croft, Joel Garner and myself. Everyone had different styles. Big Bird (Garner) was 6'8" and was impossible to get away. He didn't give up any runs. He could also bowl yorkers seemingly at will. Roberts had plenty of pace and Colin Croft was fast and bowled from wide of the crease angling the ball in, but was still capable of making it leg cut away from the batsman. He was also immensely strong and could bowl long spells, even for whole sessions. He only didn't play for long because, in the days of apartheid, he went and played in South Africa."

Whether England end up with a production line of fast bowlers remains to be seen, but for now, the fact that we have four guys capable of sustaining spells of bowling, at worst in the high eighties pace-wise, gives us grounds for optimism. At the end of this Ashes summer, whether the Aussies go home with the trophy or not, they'll certainly have a few medals of a different kind to show the folks back home.

"For me it has to be the original four of Andy Roberts, Colin Croft, Joel Garner and myself. Everyone had different styles."

GOING ON TOUR:
The Essential Barmy Army Guide To Touring
1. clear it with your family

All Out Cricket's Andy Afford picks his top four bowling performances from England's pace quartet. Well bowled indeed...

ANDREW FLINTOFF

Fred's First Five

West Indies v England at Barbados April 1-3, 2004 England 226 (Thorpe 119) and 93 for 2. West Indies 224 (Flintoff 5-58) and 94. England won by eight wickets.*

Andrew Flintoff was fast earning himself the title of England's unluckiest bowler. If a catch was to go down, it seemed unerringly that it would be Fred bowling at the time. On a fast and bouncy pitch at Bridgetown, Flintoff bowled with pace and discipline to record his first fivefer and still Test-best 5-58. The West Indies were dismissed for just over 200 and England were staring down the barrel of a hefty deficit at 155-8 until Graham Thorpe, in partnership with the tail, gained his side parity. In the second innings the Windies capitulated, with Hoggard proving the destroyer with a hat-trick comprising of Sarwan, Chanderpaul and Ryan Hinds. The defeat meant that the series was lost. And England had beaten West Indies at home for the first time in 37 years.

MATTHEW HOGGARD

Hoggy's Magnificent Seven

South Africa v England at New Wanderers Stadium, Johannesburg Jan 13-17, 2005. England 411 for 8 dec (Strauss 147, Key 83, Vaughan 82) and 332 for 9 dec (Trescothick 180). South Africa 419 (Gibbs 161, Hoggard 5-144) and 247 (Gibbs 98, Smith 67*, Hoggard 7-61). England won by 77 runs.*

Matthew Hoggard's match haul of 12-205 was some performance. With the game perfectly set up after a magnificent 180 from Marcus Trescothick, South Africa faced the prospect of seeing out the final two sessions of the match to secure a draw and head to the final match of the series 1-1. But when Jacques Kallis was dismissed first ball leaving his side on a precarious 18-3, the nerves began jangling. And when Dale Steyn edged a regulation away swinger with eight overs remaining, the game was up, with Hoggard the hero. England skipper Michael Vaughan said: "Hoggy runs through a brick wall for anyone. He's swinging the ball in these conditions, but you've still got to put it in the right areas and that's what he's doing right now. To bowl a South African team out, including nine front-line batters, in two sessions was a truly amazing effort."

The Barmy Army Symphony Orchestra

Following England around the world is a tough job...

SIMON JONES

Jonah's Test Turner

*South Africa v England St George's Park, Port Elizabeth 17-21 December, 2004. *). South Africa 337 (Dippenaar 110) and 229 (Smith 55, Kallis 61, S Jones 4-39). England 425 (Strauss 126) and 93 for 3 (Strauss 94*). England won by seven wickets*

A great match double from Andrew Strauss won him the man of the match award, but Simon Jones' second innings persistence, taking 4-39 and in the process bowling out the home side for 229, pushed home England's first dig advantage. In tropical heat, Jones sent down 13.1 overs to finish off the South African tail with a sustained spell of quick bowling. South Africa were 201-4 and looking comfortable until Jones saw off Kallis and Pollock in consecutive balls. After that it was a procession. The win meant that England had won eight Tests on the bounce.

STEPHEN HARMISON

Harmy Slips His Chain In Jamaica

West Indies v England, Kingston Jamaica, March 11-14, 2004. West Indies 311 (Smith 108, Hinds 84) and 47 all out (Harmison 7-12). England 339 (Butcher 58, Hussain 58) and 20 for 0. England won by 10 wickets.

The sight of Stephen Harmison running in to bowl with seven slips in attendance, all waiting for a seemingly inevitable edge, signified that the days of the West Indies' pace bowlers dominance over England were well and truly over. The bowling boot was now well and truly on the other foot. With the game in the balance after two innings of over 300, Hoggard and in particular Harmison, proved irresistible.

Bowling on a wicket that was tiring fast, Harmison was able to generate sufficient pace and such alarming bounce that several of the West Indies order were standing 'leg side of the ball' as opposed to right behind it. Michael Vaughan said: "Steve has produced one of the greatest spells of bowling by an England player."

> "Steve has produced one of the greatest spells of bowling by an England player."

the npower girls
2006

npower **6**

npower Test Series

34

things you
always wanted
to know about Fred
but were afraid
to ask

MANCHESTER UNITED OR A NIGHT AT THE OPERA? MODERN MUSIC OR THE OLD STUFF? GOOD BRAINS OR GOOD LOOKS? FRED GIVES IT TO US STRAIGHT, CONFIRM-ING, DENYING AND DOTTING THE 'I'S AND CROSSING THE 'T'S ON EVERYTHING YOU COULD EVER WANT TO KNOW. ALL OUT CRICKET'S IAN SYKES SAT DOWN WITH THE MAN IN MUMBAI...

AS A YOUTH...

I think I read somewhere that you were a good chess player as a junior – did you have a pre-ferred opening that you would look to play?

I played for Lancashire when I was about 11 but I didn't have a set opening move, I was a bit of a mav-erick to be honest. Haven't played for ages actually.

Have you ever had a go on a motorbike?

Yeah, when I was a kid I rode one on the grass in the park in Lytham. I didn't nick it though, it was one of those that you could hire out for a quid or something like that. I don't think I've been on one since. Not like Hoggy. (This would all change after Mumbai...)

Where you ever a Joe Bloggs-wearing Manc?

No way, I'm not a Manc for a start. I'm a Preston lad, let's make that quite clear. Although I'm pretty sure me brother used to wear a few Joe Bloggs things...

What's the best Christmas present you've ever had?

A Spectrum 48k computer. No doubt about it. I remember being chuffed to

bits with that, good piece of kit, it was.

Have you ever been in a fight?

I'm not a fighter, no. I might have had the odd scrape when I was eight or nine but nothing serious. I don't really like the idea of being hit, as much as anything.

Did you ever have a space hopper?

Oh yeah, when I was 19 [laughs]. No, I had one when I was about four or five but I can't remember much about it.

"Now Freddie, what have I told you?
You can't score runs in the pavilion...

MUSIC...

What's the most expensive bit of memorabilia you own, and what is it worth?
I've got a signed gold disc of Elvis' single 'Loving You'. I bought it from a collector, it was quite expensive, but you know, it's Elvis isn't it.

If you had to take five favourite records to a desert island what would they be?
This might take a little while.....
Rocket Man – Elton John
Someone Like You – Rod Stewart
Burning Love – Elvis
Fly Me To The Moon – Frank Sinatra
Wonderwall – Oasis

Is there any contemporary music that you like?
I mostly listen to Elvis, Elton John and all that older stuff I grew up with, but yeah, I do like some of the modern stuff although I couldn't start to tell you what was in the charts, mind. I don't really take all that stuff in.

Who are your favourite band?
Dunno really, Oasis are up there.

What's the song you hate the most?
Beautiful by James Blunt. What a terrible track.

EATING AND DRINKING...

If you were only allowed two beverages for the rest of your life and one of them was water, what would the other one be?
Vimto. It reminds me of when I was growing up 'cos I've always loved it since I was a kid. We used to make ice pops out of the stuff.

"Some woman asked me to sign her breasts in Sydney when I was fielding for the World XI against Australia. I couldn't do it though, it just wasn't right."

What food do you miss most when you're on tour?

Fish fingers, chips and beans with bread and butter. No sauce, 'cos you've got your beans. I'll have that when I get home, just make loads of butties.

What's the first thing you take out of the fridge when you get back home from a tour?

If it's night-time, it'll be a beer. If it's morning, it'll be the bacon to make some bacon butties. So beer or bacon.

What's your favourite hangover cure?

I never get hangovers [smiles], I don't drink that much...

FANS...
What's the oddest thing that a fan has ever done?

Some woman asked me to sign her breasts in Sydney when I was fielding for the World XI against Australia. I couldn't do it though, it just wasn't right. Could you imagine having your picture taken with them?

What do you think of the Barmy Army?

I love them, they give us great support wherever we are and that's a real plus for a side. I've got to be honest though, there are times after a day's play when you go for a meal and you really don't want to bump into a crowd that's been on the pop all day.

Best Barmy Army story?

There are two lads who go everywhere dressed as Sylvester the Cat and Pink Panther, and one night in Pakistan I borrowed the Sylvester costume and joined up with the rest of the team. I started acting up and stuff and the lads didn't realise it was me for about an hour.

CRICKET...
How often do you wash your kit?

Not as often as I should, you know. I aim to get it done after each day's play but I'm a bit slack really.

What gives you the most pleasure – making a hundred, or bowling a 12-over spell and taking five wickets?
I see myself as a batsman who bowls a bit, so it's got to be scoring a hundred – that's a great feeling.

Are you aware of the 'mince' you do with your back leg after hitting a good shot – it makes me howl, a big bloke like yourself.
I'm not having it. No-one's ever raised it with me before. That's wrong, no mince. No way.

In the future, can you imagine yourself playing for England as just a batsman?
Possibly yes. A lot depends on how my body holds up. I really enjoy bowling so I'd like to keep chucking it down for as long as I'm playing cricket but it depends how the body wears.

Why are you dropping catches now?
Well I went through a bad patch as people sometimes do in the slips. It's funny, I can't really explain it but I've had a few stick over here in India so I reckon I've turned the corner now.

Dinner party – your three all-time favourite guests?
Elvis, Sinatra and my mate Paddy (former Lancashire opener, Patrick McKeown). Be a good night that.

In a flash restaurant you notice you haven't been charged for that last bottle of wine. Do you tell the waitress, or let it go?
Thank you very much, cheers love.

ABOUT FRED...

What's the best/worst thing about being a dad?
The best thing is just having a family and being with them, it means everything. But the worst thing for me is being away from home, like now. Obviously it's particularly hard at the moment because it feels like everyone's seen Corey except for me. We're lucky to earn a living from playing cricket but it's very hard being away from the family for long periods.

Would you prefer to be really clever, or really handsome?
Ooh I dunno [turns to Kevin Pietersen]
AF: KP would you rather be really clever or really good-looking?
KP: Easy, I'm already really good-looking, and I'm happy the way I am.
AF: Aye, a bit dim though. I think I'd rather meet each one halfway, a bit of a cop out I know, but half and half.

What will you be doing when you're 45?
Not much I hope. I've not really given it too much thought yet, too busy getting on with what's going on now.

You're given one ticket for the opera and one for Manchester United, what would you watch?
I'm not a big opera fan but I'd give it a bash. I'd rather stick pins in my eyes than go and watch Man U. I'm a City man, me.

BEST AND WORST OF FRED...

What's your least favourite sport?
Athletics – it's just so boring.

What's the worst film you've ever seen?
Oh I watched one the other day, and it was awful – Donnie Brasco. Nothing happened. I was sat there waiting for it to kick in and nothing – what a waste of time.

You can bring one fictional character to life – who?
Erm, Yoda. I'd take him to the Friargate Social Club in Preston and introduce him to the lads. He could show us all how to use the force and stuff.

Your favourite Viz character?
Fat Slags [laughs his head off].

DOWNING STREET...

Did you really make Blair get the beers in?
Yeah, he asked me if I wanted a drink and I fancied a beer so that was that. Tony produced the goods, good lad.

Taken from All Out Cricket magazine, available from WHSmith or subscribe at www.alloutcricket.co.uk

BARMY COMMENT:
Fearlessness

Our Man In The Stands turns the flood lights on England's new attitude to cricket. Somehow playing the game as if it is only a game...

Absence of fear. Or, if 'absence' is too strong, then, let's say, manageable fear.

That, I think, has been the major difference in this new England side - they seem to treat a Test match as if - ho hum - it's just another game, and to bat and bowl as if the whole thing's fun.

Now, this doesn't seem a big deal, put bluntly, but the ability to reproduce your best form when there's such an enormous amount riding on it - plus, a stadium full of fanatics watching your every move - and - on top of that - an ultra slo-mo camera focused on your every blink and twitch - well, it's what, it seems to me, top class sport is all about.

Now, I hasten to add - no - I don't know what the hell I'm talking about - not having played cricket anywhere much above your average Park scenario. (Games where you had to be careful where you hit it - just in case you beaned one of those kids on the swings and slides, or K.O.'d that old woman with her dog, and her shopping bag.)

So, I admit it, I'm guessing. It's supposition. But I used to get nervous waiting to bat against Old Draconian's Thirds, for Heaven's sake, so what it must be like, say, at Lord's - God knows!

But, if I am qualified to comment on such lofty matters, it's due to the fact that I've watched, believe me, a shed-load of sport, a whole 'Kentucky Fried Chicken' bucket-load of it. I think, in fact, that I was born on a sofa. With a remote control clutched in my tiny mitts, my parents looking on proudly as I flicked from channel to channel.

Plus - if, like me, you think the bulk of a Newspaper is there to give you something to rest the Sports pages on, then you understand that I've read a fair bit of commentary too.

So - back to the point at issue - nerves, and the ability to control them.

This, I think, is where Michael Vaughan comes in. His mantra has been 'play your normal game. If it's there to hit, then give it a go.' This has meant, of course, that watching the modern English Test match is about as restful as having your teeth pulled, and the average Test lasts three days and not five, but it is - I think we all agree - entertaining!

Perhaps the only down side of this approach is the effect on Vaughan's personal form and batting average. Because he instils this 'gung ho' approach in his troops, he can't very well be seen to go out there and prod

"Kevin Pieterson, for instance, gives off the impression that the only time he gets nervous is when they take the Hair Dryer off his bonce and he checks to see how the dye has taken."

"Incidentally - my vote for the most nerveless batsman of our generation? For me - David Gower. A man who always seemed to bat as if he was on the veranda holding a dry martini."

it around like Chris Tavare's timid younger brother. No, he has to set an example - get after it! This is why, I believe, he unleashes those trademark Off Drives just a wee bit too soon in his innings - with the consequence that he is averaging thirty seven or so since becoming Captain, as opposed to somewhere nearer fifty before.

But - I'd argue - small price to pay.

Of course, this new steely England mentality is a lot to do with personnel as well. Kevin Pieterson, for instance, gives off the impression that the only time he gets nervous is when they take the Hair Dryer off his bonce and he checks to see how the dye has taken. Also, Andrew Strauss. If he wasn't batting you feel that he'd be in some boardroom somewhere selling stocks and shares, or firing some subordinate.

(Incidentally - my vote for the most nerveless batsman of our generation? For me - David Gower. A man who always seemed to bat as if he was on the veranda holding a dry martini.)

But - if there are nerveless characters, then there are those for whom it seems that facing Test match bowling is about as much fun as facing your average firing squad. The jury is still out on Ian Bell, but I have a suspicion that he could be from the Mark Ramprakash school of relaxation, and not, say, your Kevin Pieterson type.

I mention Ramprakash because of the horrors of watching him bat for England on so many occasions. It was like watching your kid in the bean bag race in the school sports, willing him to do well, but knowing - all the while - that he's going to fall over his feet and make a tits of the whole business.

Ramprakash - arguably the most talented County batsman of our time - just couldn't relax.

The bat in his hand seemed like it was welded to his gloves.

He reminded me of a mate of mine who played jazz saxophone. You'd speak to him before he was about to play live, and - for the life of him - he couldn't get a word out. He was rigid with tension. He'd grunt, and that was it. With the result, of course, that when he came to play the smooth fluid jazz style it tended to sound, well, like the morning-after one too many pints of Youngs Mixed.

The trouble with batting is - you have to stay still. There's nowhere for all that pent up nervous energy to go. If you're a rugby player, say, or a footballer - at least you can run about, clatter into someone - that always helps. Cricket - you've just got to stand there and take it. (The exception that proves the rule, of course - Derek "twitching maniac" Randall!)

So - if Michael Vaughan has in some way managed to make the English changing room less like the Colosseum just before the matinee performance of the Christians versus the Lions, then more power to his leading elbow.

All hail, Michael Vaughan!

YOUR MAN IN THE STANDS

THE ROUND

It was the golden age of the all-rounder, and through the eighties debates raged from the bars of fulham to the bazaars of faisalabad – who was the greatest, Botham or Imran? And what about Kapil? Or Hadlee? If Sir Garfield was King, who should accede? Since then we've seen Kallis, Cairns and Pollock vie for the crown, but only one other can truly join the round table. The question is, among the modern greats, where does Andrew Flintoff sit? All Out Cricket's Phil Walker compares the big one to the big four.

TABLE

IMRAN KHAN

88 Tests, average 37.69, six hundreds, 18 fifties, HS 136 / 362 wickets at 22.81 (1971-1992)
One of those shimmering human specimens for whom life has come far too easily. Imran was the most complete cricketer of his generation. As the iconic captain who beat England on their own patch in 1987 (at Headingley, 7-40 in the one result of the summer) and who later led Pakistan to World Cup glory, Imran was also the period's most stirring figurehead. As a batsman Imran played as he lived, with great style and resolve. He could whack it, deflect it, block the life out of it. His average is the best of the four, because whereas the others hit themselves out of a hole, Imran never gave anything away, his exulted position in Pakistan life preventing casual flirtations with anything fast and loose (at least on the pitch). And what a bowler. The grand, arching action, the sudden jut wide of the crease replete with hold-your-breath mid-air pause before delivery, and the original toe-cruncher to follow...that was Imran.

THE MOMENT:
1992 World Cup, and Pakistan are a mess. Imran returns halfway through, and a ragbag bunch of in-fighters are transformed. He tells them to fight like tigers, and they scrap their way to the final, where Imran makes runs, takes wickets, inspires Wasim Akram, and lifts aloft both the cup and a nation's self-respect.

IF HE WAS A NOVEL...
Pride and Prejudice – Jane Austen. Dashing, unbuttoned hero overcomes fiercely partisan culture to win the day...

SUMMARY:
Batting 8; Bowling 9; Charisma rating: 9. Total 26.
Pretty, good.

IAN BOTHAM

102 Tests, average 33.54, 14 hundreds, 22 fifties, HS 208 / 383 wickets at 28.40 (1977-1992)
Ah, Beefy. Where to start? Rather like Dylan's motorcycle accident in 1966 when the acolytes thought him dead, if Botham had gone out at the top in, say 1985, he would have sat one along from Sir Garfield at the round table. Problem was, injury and blond streaks got in the way, and we found he was mortal after all. But this shouldn't cloud that period between his debut five-wickets against Australia in 1977 and the murderous fourteenth Test hundred at Brisbane in 1986, a time when Botham was English cricket. As a young bowler he was irresistible, a snake-hipped tyro with pace, brio, and an unplayable outswinger. And he clearly loved batting – all the old footage chimes with Flintoff now, because both men spend half their time laughing. Headingley '81 is just Botham and Dilley having a giggle. But he could bat as well as hit, and would have averaged 40 if he was a lesser bowler. And although stats won't do for Botham, that one that reads 14 hundreds from number six is still utterly staggering. The omnipotent West Indians were the only team to tame him – he averaged just 21 in 20 matches.

THE MOMENT:
1981. You really should know by now.

IF HE WAS A NOVEL...
The Call Of The Wild – Jack London. The wild man of English cricket, scrapping like a dog 'til the last...

SUMMARY:
Batting: 8; Bowling: 8: Charisma Factor: 9. Total: 25.
Charisma would be a ten, but for that blond mullet and striped blazer effort circa '85.

KAPIL DEV

131 Tests, average 31.05, eight hundreds, 27 fifties, HS 163 / 434 wickets at 29.64 (1978-1994)
Kapil Dev's greatest achievement was to devise a gameplan on the deadest tracks in the game whilst maintaining the stamina and motivation to somehow reach 400 wickets. The old boy was barely standing at the end, but what an effort. With the bat he was devastating in short bursts. Eight tons is a fair reflection of his approach – the chiselled hundred was Sunil's job – but when the wind blew his way, balls went long. Kapil's essence was captured at Lord's in 1990 after Gooch's 333. India needed 24 to avoid the follow-on with Narendra Hirwani, the world's best number 11, in his bottle tops at the other end. Eddie Hemmings is bowling. Balls one and two are circumspectly blocked. Balls three to six are circumspectly mullered over Eddie's head. On commentary Benaud is unmoved: "I suppose it's only logical. If you need 24 to avoid the follow-on, why not get it in four hits?" Next ball Hirwani is lbw.

The Moment:
1983 at Ahmedabad, versus West Indies. 40 degree heat, best to get

back in the shade, so Kapil takes nine wickets in the innings. India still lose.

If He Was A Novel...
On The Road – Jack Kerouac. 16 years on Indian pitches? Kapil just loved pounding the tarmac...

Summary:
Batting: 7; Bowling: 9; Charisma Rating: 7. Total: 23.
Good moustache in his favour, voluptuous, top-heavy action a minor hindrance (not so much chest-on as chest-out), adoration of a billion Indians a definite plus.

RICHARD HADLEE

86 Tests, average 27.16, two hundreds, 15 fifties, HS 151* / 431 wickets at 22.29 (1973-1990)
Stern, humourless, driven, brilliant. When Beefy's bag probably featured a decaying jockstrap and a nicked bat, Hadlee's coffin contained a list of goals and targets written neatly on a piece of A4. It was this single-mindedness, allied to the purest bowling action in history and an alchemist's control over a cricket ball's mysterious properties that made Hadlee the first man to 400. 36 times he took five wickets, in 86 matches. Not express pace, by keeping a few revs in hand he gave the ball time to banana all over the place, all with complete control. As a batsman he was the weakest of all the great all-rounders, but still a dangerous left-handed hitter, whose penchant for smashing the opposition's fast bowlers told us something about the inner entertainer lurking beneath that iceman exterior.

The Moment:
Last Test, England, 1990. A masterclass, 5-53, and a wicket with his very last delivery. Still striving, still brilliant.

If He Was A Novel...
The Big Sleep – Raymond Chandler. Sharp, coldly clinical. Forensically inspecting the batsman for chinks, weaknesses and half-truths. Hadlee, the Philip Marlowe of fast bowling.

Summary:
Batting: 6; Bowling: 10; Charisma factor: 5. Total: 21
Too damned predictable, too remorseless. Everything was in order, all the time, and it drained the romantic. But then who needs charisma when you take a wicket every 50 balls?

ANDREW FLINTOFF

59 Tests, average 33.47, five hundreds, 22 fifties, HS 167 / 174 wickets at 31.45 (1998-)
As fans we remember matches, not numbers, and in under 60 Tests Flintoff has built up a portfolio of seminal moments to warrant a place at the round table. And where other great all-rounders wilted with age, Flintoff seems to get better. Today there is no better bruising fast bowler around. He never gets hit, never bowls a bad spell. He doesn't have the eight-fers that others cling to, but he is relentless, and takes wickets for those at the other end, working as part of a unit that shares its wickets rather than a sole spearhead in the Hadlee/Kapil mould. He looks and acts like a batsman, plays straight, is tight in defence, and rarely fails to contribute. He made at least a half-century in eight consecutive Tests in 2004. He is now making runs everywhere. He can, believe it, be relied upon, and that was something even his staunchest supporters never thought they'd say. In two years we might be talking about England's greatest ever cricketer.
We might even be talking about him now. Even Botham would agree that one thing is for sure: another starring Ashes win, in Australia, and all bets are off. Then there's the World Cup, and Flintoff also happens to be the best one-day cricketer on earth. Interesting times.

The Moment:
Saturday 6 August 2005, England v Australia, Edgbaston. Do or die. Saviour or fall guy. Flintoff hits four sixes (nine in the match) in a last-ditch 72 from 181 all out, and an hour later, delivers the greatest over in Ashes history. English cricket is back.

If He Was A Novel...
Man and Superman – George Bernard Shaw. Ok, it's a play but it does sum Fred up. Salt of the earth, human, approachable. Talent beyond compare, saviour of the nation.

Summary:
Batting: 9; Bowling: 8; Charisma Factor: 10. Total 27 (to be continued...)
He made cricket good again.

THE SWING KINGS

5 Irfan Pathan (India)
What makes Pathan so dangerous is his left-handedness. Quicker than he looks, Pathan swings the ball in late to the right-handed batsman, always attacking the stumps, making the batsman work hard. Although inexperienced, many good judges reckon Pathan to be India's next great all-rounder.

4 Fidel Edwards (West Indies)
Edwards' unorthodoxy, although rendering him injury-prone, makes him a most dangerous opponent. High pace, combined with an unrefined slinger's action, combine to provide a genuine physical challenge when the ball is dug in short and a wicket-taking threat when it is pitched up.

3 Shoaib Akhtar (Pakistan)
In 2005's County Championship, playing for Worcestershire, Shoaib Akhtar looked more 'Puffing Billy' than the much-hyped 'Rawalpindi Express'

of yore. With fitness levels looking lower than normal, Akhtar was regularly able to get through four quick overs, but rarely five. At his best Akhtar is a fine sight. Charging in a full 40 metres to deliver both in and outswinging thunderbolts that shatter stumps and metatarsals in equal measure. On his day Akhtar is irresistible. Not at his best, he can prove a liability.

2 Chaminda Vaas (Sri Lanka)
Steadiness personified. Not blessed with extreme pace, Chaminda Vaas has to be one of the most difficult bowlers to get after in the world game. Vaas mixes swingers, slower balls, bouncers and cutters to create a bowling style that renders all batsmen

watchful. In helpful conditions he can be devastating, producing late inswing to trap right-handers LBW. If there is less in the pitch, he's still likely to provide control for his captain even when conditions are at their hardest.

1 Matthew Hoggard (England)
England's king of the swingers, Matthew Hoggard has proved himself invaluable for Michael Vaughan over the last three years. Since debut in 2000, he has rarely disappointed with the new ball, and if conditions are favourable his boundless stamina and work ethic makes his a captain's dream. Another swing bowler who is quicker than he looks, Hoggard has proved to be one of very few swing bowlers who is as effective bowling at left-handers as he is right. England's workhorse and the Barmy Army's 'Jungle VIP'.

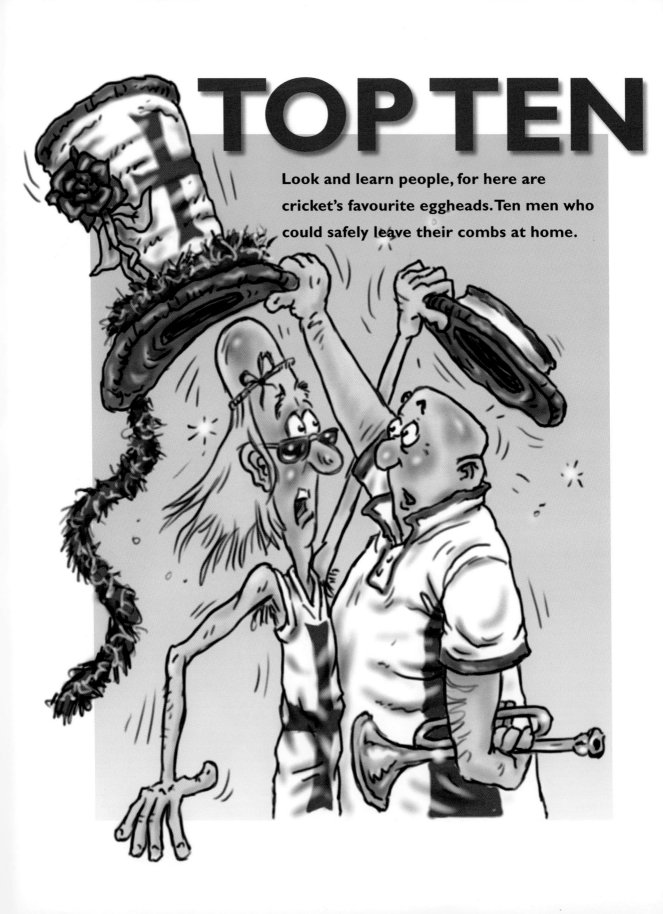

TOP TEN

Look and learn people, for here are cricket's favourite eggheads. Ten men who could safely leave their combs at home.

Bald Cricketers!

GREG MATTHEWS
**Australia,
33 Tests, 1983-1993**

New South Wales' off-spinning batsman, Greg Matthews played in Allan Border's much-beaten Australia side of the eighties and always bowled in a cap and sweater – we now know why he kept on the headgear. But Matthews' is a story of triumph over 'hair-dversity' as he very publicly beat the drum for the Melbourne hair replacement clinic, Advances Hair Studio. Martin Crowe, Graham Gooch and Shane Warne have since followed (hir)suit(e). Greg Matthews – the man who launched a thousand weaves.

HERSCHELLE GIBBS
**South Africa
70 Tests, 1996-?**

When Gary 'Bald Eagle' Kirsten hung up his rainbow nation bandana in 2004, it fell to Herschelle Gibbs to fly the flag for 'bliskops' throughout South Africa. The diamond stud and skinhead, although offering a degree of camouflage, don't fully obscure the fact that Herschelle has a head that looks as smooth as a baby's bottom.

England player Q&A's

SIMON JONES

BEST KEEPER

Hands	Andrew Flintoff
Speed	Devon Smith (WI)
Athleticism	Herschelle Gibbs (SA) Paul Collingwood
Reactions	Ricky Ponting (AUS)

> "He's possibly most 'fondly' remembered for shaving his head on England's 1993/94 tour of the Caribbean, only to suffer sun-stroke."

CHRIS LEWIS
**England,
32 Tests, 1990-1996**

The much-derided England all-rounder is famous within cricket for many things largely unrelated to his sport.

He's possibly most 'fondly' remembered for shaving his head on England's 1993/94 tour of the Caribbean, only to suffer sun-stroke.

BRIAN CLOSE
England, 22 Tests, 1949-1976

Rarely has such an expanse of baldness been worn with such conviction. Yorkshire, Somerset, Arsenal, Bradford City & England are but a few of the sides on the legendary hardman's CV. One of sport's most colourful characters, Close is famously credited with many things. For taking on the world's fastest bowlers wearing little more than a stiff brimmed cap and a handkerchief in the trouser pocket. For mentoring the youthful Ian Botham when a fledgling West Countryman. And finally, for fancying himself as being 'a bit handy' when publicly stating that he considered himself to be a match for the world heavyweight boxing champion of the day – one Muhammad Ali. Brian Close… no shrinking violet.

JAMES ANDERSON

PERSONAL

Favourite film	Happy Gilmore
Favourite record	Laid – James
Non-sporting hero	My dad
Football team	Arsenal
Golf handicap	12
Biggest fear	Spiders, Sharks
School subject	PE, Maths, English
First job	Ticket sales – Burnley F.C.
Cricket idol	Peter Martin
First ashes memory	Botham's Ashes – on video
Dream car	Porsche 911
Holiday destination	The Maldives
Favourite food	Shepherds Pie (Mum's)
Clothing brand	Not fussy

SIR VIVIAN RICHARDS
West Indies,
121 Tests, 1974-1991

The greatest, most influential cricketer of all time? At the crease – superhuman. In the field – brooding and enigmatic. Off the field – wildly charismatic. Such is the presence of Richards, his hair loss only added to the distinguished nature of his appearance – almost as though he went bald on purpose.

VINTCENT VAN DER BIJL
Middlesex, Natal & Transvaal
1967-1983

Vintcent van der Bijl played his entire first-class cricket during South Africa's period of sporting isolation, rendering him possibly the best player never to play Test cricket. An enormously tall and thick-set quick bowler, van der Bijl was headmasterly in appearance and headmasterly by nature. And why wouldn't he be – he was at one time a headmaster.

TONY GREIG
England, 58, Tests, 1972-1977

The charismatic South African-born Greig burst onto the international cricket scene in the early seventies as a swashbuckling right-handed batsman, master slip catcher and right-arm swing or spin bowler. And not only did he play the part, he looked it. Tall, blond and handsome in his youth, almost Tarzan-like in appearance, 'Greigy' appeared to be the sort of bloke that if asked, would…

As a player he's best remembered for orchestrating the defection of cricket's cream to Kerry Packer's World Series and for decreeing that, as England captain, he would make Clive Lloyd's mighty West Indies side of 1976, grovel. England lost the 5-Test series 3-0. Nowadays the 59 year-old Channel 9 commentator lives in Australia, is as bald as a badger and has found fame/infamy due largely to his energetic pronouncement at the fall of a wicket of "Goodnight Charlie!" Apparently it signifies that the batsman is out…

DARREN LEHMANN
Australia,
28 Tests, 1998-2004

The first cricketer to wear the Shrek monicker (and with good reason), Darren Lehmann has proved a huge figure in Australian domestic cricket for decades. Bursting onto the scene as a precociously talented junior, it was only in has latter years that his first-class record was converted into Test runs. Originally a dashing left-hander, as his hairline receded so did the number of rash shots he played, and he ended his career in the game's top flight with an average above 44. He ended his spell in the Australian side by offering to step aside for another wunderkind, Michael Clarke. Lehmann is now a popular member of the Sky Sports commentary team.

SYED KIRMANI
India, 88 Tests, 1976-1986

India wicketkeeper Syed Kirmani certainly stood out from his compatriots during a distinguished international career that spanned a decade. Kirmani, a deeply religious man, would shave his head before undertaking any tour, with his clean pate offering proof for his dear old mum at home that he was pure of mind, body and soul. Kirmani is currently India's chairman of selectors.

KIM BARNETT
England, 4 Test, 1988-1989

Obviously number one...
An idiosyncratic right-handed opening batsman, who seemingly took guard behind the square leg umpire before shuffling into line, Kim Barnett played for Derbyshire and Gloucestershire with distinction between 1979-2002. A prolific county cricketer throughout his career, and someone who fell into the category of 'could have played more for his country'. His 'one-off' stance at the crease, combined with a handlebar moustache and colossal bald head made Staffordshire-born Barnett one of the domestic game's most recognisable figures.
And anyone who goes by the name of 'Barnett' and has a head that looks like polished mahogany has to see the irony…surely?

"Such is the presence of Richards, his hair loss only added to the distinguished nature of his appearance – almost as though he went bald on purpose."

GOING ON TOUR:
The Essential Barmy Army Guide To Touring
2. check your accomodation is o.k.

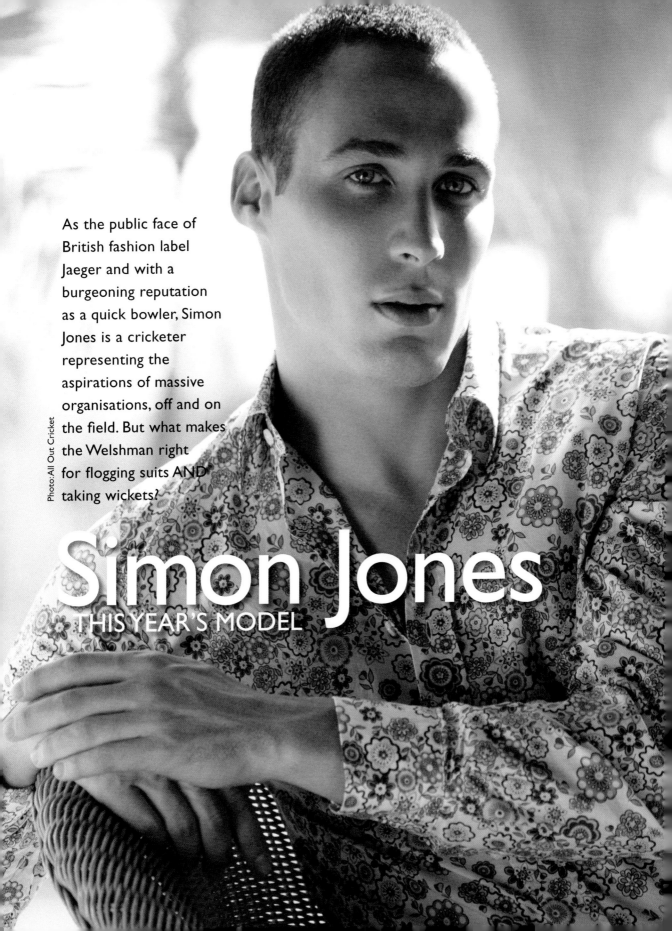

As the public face of British fashion label Jaeger and with a burgeoning reputation as a quick bowler, Simon Jones is a cricketer representing the aspirations of massive organisations, off and on the field. But what makes the Welshman right for flogging suits AND taking wickets?

Simon Jones
THIS YEAR'S MODEL

Brad Pitt, Jake Gyllenhall, Orlando Bloom, Johnny Depp, Clive Owen, Jose Mourinho, Shayne Ward, Daniel Craig… SIMON JONES. According to over 100,000 female readers polled in *New Woman* magazine, these men rate as the fittest of the fit and the top nine sexiest men in the world. Elsewhere within the hot 100, Thierry Henry va va voomed in at 12, David Beckham number 14, Jonny Wilkinson 28 and Our Fred ranked a more than creditable, some say charitable, 54th. It would appear that the readership just couldn't get enough sporting totty in 2005.

Back in April, incoming ECB chief executive David Collier set out several specific aims within his strategic plan for advancing cricket's ongoing popularity. One of which was to have three England cricketers recognisable to 10% of the population by 2009. Already, in Michael Vaughan, Kevin Pietersen and Andrew Flintoff, he appears well ahead of schedule. And in Simon Jones he has someone else with the potential to raise the bar still higher.

Currently ranked 17 in the ICC World Bowler Ratings, the 27 year-old Jones has taken the game by storm in the past nine months. His testosterone-fuelled swing bowling, macho celebrations, crop-haired good looks and mass Ashes exposure has

elevated the man from the valleys away from the sports pages and into the gossip columns.

A PR contract with Evolution Model and Talent Management and under the wing of agent Charles Collymore at CS Sport Management, Jones' profile has shot even higher. Recently, the 6'3" Welshman has been featured on the cover of the *Evening Standard* as one of the paper's men of the moment, as a naked centrefold in women's lifestyle bible *Cosmopolitan,* and on the back of his ever-burgeoning reputation as a cricketer and boy about town, has become the face (and body) of high-end fashion label, Jaeger.

Catherine Thomas, Jaeger marketing director, saw the game of cricket as the initial attractor and catalyst for her company becoming involved with Jones: "Why Simon? Well, he represents a sport that, like Jaeger, is quintessentially British. This, along with his love of Jaeger suits in particular, and fashion in general, we feel makes for a fantastic partnership. Commitment-wise, Simon is helping us promote the brand, specifically Jaeger

Menswear, over the course of this year. Whether we continue longterm depends very much on our customers' reactions, and early indications are very positive."

But what does he think about it all – is he now all mouth and trousers? Apparently not: "It's all good fun, but I'm a cricketer," said Jones, "I've got where I am through my cricket and that's what I do. It's cool, all of the other stuff that I get to do and a way of earning extra money in a short career. But it's basically good fun.

"I get offered lots of stuff, but I only do some of it. I've turned down a few TV shows and the likes – I turn it down if I think that there's a chance I might make a tit of myself. (Laughs)

"I get offered lots of stuff, but I only do some of it. I've turned down a few TV shows and the likes – I turn it down if I think that there's a chance I might make a tit of myself. (Laughs) So I've turned down quite a few of those things!"

So I've turned down quite a few of those things!"

Jones has joined a select band of performers that appear to transcend their sport's individual appeal. David Beckham, possibly the most recognised sports star in the world today, has his own Instinct brand aftershave. He endorses Police sunglasses, Adidas sportswear and honours a myriad of Far Eastern contracts, providing the benchmark by which a British athlete's marketability and fame is measured.

Tennis' 'Tiger' Tim Henman flogs washing powder on the back of the prospect of him getting your whites white enough to match his image; rugby's Jonny Wilkinson is another champion whose wholesome English gentleman image is seen as the ideal match with upper crust clothing brand, Hackett. And Jones offers something very similar for Jaeger. Catherine Thomas was again very candid in assessing the appeal of sportsmen to potential customers: "Why do top flight athletes make attractive propositions for clothing brands? Because they are top-achievers in their own right and have strong popular appeal…Oh, and they have excellent physiques!"

Prior to Jones' breakthrough summer of 2005, that excellent physique was not as it should be. Injury and missed opportunity had seen the Swansea-born, Llanelli-raised quick bowler more a member of the supporting cast than a genuine centre-stager. Returning last winter, on tour in South Africa after a long lay-off following knee surgery, he showed glimpses of what he was capable of. His four late wickets in the second innings of the Port Elizabeth Test turned around a match that was creeping away from his side, giving England a series lead they were not

to relinquish. He finished third in the tour averages with 15 scalps, behind Andrew Flintoff and Matthew Hoggard, but bowled far fewer overs than England's top pair or fourth ranked bowler, Stephen Harmison.

It was also the manner in which Michael Vaughan appeared to use him, only bowling him when options seemed limited and a 'roll of the dice' necessary. Simon Jones was, on that tour, the last stop on the line. A bit erratic, occasionally expensive and looking unsure as to whether he should bowl flat out or look to contain. But after 2005's heroics, Jones now finds himself elevated from England sideman to 'go-to-guy', offering his captain blistering speed, accuracy and the most-hyped of all cricketing grails, reverse swing.

The summer saw him outbowl all-comers, finishing as the top seamer in either side's averages, amid a cast of luminaries. His displays at Trent

"All the Ashes it was the best I'd felt in England colours. The Australians seem to bring the best out in you and it was first time that I was really showing what I could do."

Bridge and Old Trafford in particular, were textbook exhibitions of the fast bowler's art, before cramp at Manchester and the onset of an ankle problem at Nottingham saw him leave the field in both games.

First innings figures in both rubbers of 6-53 and 5-44 were impressive, but it was the sole second innings dismissal at OT that proved one of the series' biggest talking points. Michael Clarke was the batsman. It was mid-afternoon and the precocious right hander had curbed the flamboyance normally associated with his batting, favouring a fluent but more considered second fiddle approach in support of

his skipper, Ricky Ponting.

Ponting was saving the game for his team and only needed a sideman to see them the rest of the way home for the draw. Jones was bowling beautifully. Each ball clocked at around the 85mph mark, some arcing away; some dipping in. And it was the discipline with which the bowler maintained a three to six inch line outside off stump that was most impressive. In that corridor, the ball was perfectly placed to perform either of the tasks Jones might set it. After a succession of perfect away swingers, Jones produced a ball that ducked back late to flatten off stump with Clarke stranded, offering no

stroke, bat held aloft. When batting, it is said that there are only two categories by which to measure shouldering arms – they're either good leaves (ball misses stumps) or bad ones (ball doesn't). This most definitely fell into the latter.

But it was the previous examination set Clarke that made it even more crippling. It wasn't a miracle ball delivered as a bolt from the blue – the sort of ball that Fidel Edwards produces for West Indies every ten over and 55 runs conceded. It was part of a sustained piece of bowling that saw the coming of age of Simon Jones and the return to the classroom of another young cricketer. With that delivery and that passage of play, Jones had arrived.

But where had it come from? He'd bowled quickly and without luck at Lord's (2-48 and 1-69). Three more wickets came during the 'thriller down the Villa' in Edgbaston, but it all clicked into place in the north-west during the third Test. Why the change? Jones picks up the story: "To be honest with you, I'd felt good in all of the games last summer. I'd had some stick in the press, people questioning whether I was this, or that. But in all the Ashes it was the best I'd felt in England colours. The Australians seem to bring the best out in you and it was first time that I was really showing what I could do."

With the cricket seemingly on the up and up, marrying his life off and on the field is going to be a challenge. He's visited Marrakesh to shoot the pictures you see in this feature as part of Jaeger's spring and summer clothes collection ((should we cut this?)) and even managed to shoehorn in a high-profile holiday in Los Angeles with fellow blade Pietersen as a guest of actor, Mickey Rourke. Not to mention the ticker-tape reception in Trafalgar Square, the awarding of an MBE and subsequent trip to Buckingham Palace. It was on his way home from receiving his honour from the Queen that we caught up with Jones, in the midst of an exacting schedule of interviews and press calls in advance of the Sunday departure for India. Jones was still on a high from the morning's events: "Days like these don't come around that often. All the boys were buzzing about it."

And what of his elevation to the status of one of the world's most eligible bachelors – has the reaction of team-mates been as supportive? "A few of them have been calling me 'Top Ten' and it's all a good laugh. But to be honest with you, although you list all that stuff, my winter has been pretty boring really! Most of my time has been spent up at Loughborough. I've been getting back to full fitness. It's what you have to do if you want to play sport and I desperately want to play international cricket.

"It was good to go out to Marrakesh on that job, it was only done over a weekend, but it made a nice break away from training. It was a cool place, sunny and all tha', but not so much for me. The people were nice and the girl I worked with on the shoot, she was a Russian supermodel called Natalia Semanova and she has been modelling for 12 years since she moved to New York when she was 14. It was good to talk to her about things, she was really laid-back."

And with this extra media attention, there will be potential for complications and compromises and there will be hurdles to navigate. But they are all the sort of barriers that most of us wouldn't mind a crack at. And with good advice, a clear head and hopefully the end of his injury hassles, England may, as they head for Australia after this summer, be about to have four of the world's top ten bowlers in their team. Obviously, it's not the most sexy poll to top, but there are worse things in life. Simon Jones eh, who would have thought it? ●

SPEAKY'S CORNER

HARMONY HISTORIES
SA 95/96 ONWARDS

PART TWO

BC: The next tour. South African. 95/96.

Leafy: Unfortunately, the main songs from that Tour can't be printed, for reasons of taste.

BC: Why were the songs more, let's say, to the point than the Ashes songs?

Leafy: Yes, very much to the point and although they were strongly worded the Afrikaans had no problem with this.

BC: Is there anything we can print?

Leafy: The '10 Rand to the Pound' song was used a lot. 'Everywhere we go' was regularly sung. There were also a lot of pro-England team songs, with Robin Smith the hero and crowd favourite on his return to his native South Africa, and particularly Durban.

BC: Where do you stand on swearing in songs?

Leafy: From the beginning we were praised for not swearing and have tried to influence people that way, particularly through the Songs of Praise/Barmy Harmonies; the bottom line is that you cannot tell people what to sing. Personally, however, I think that the songs come over much better through the use of our wit and humour rather than resorting to swearing.

BC: But it was in other ways a memorable series?

Leafy: Yes, in lots of ways, the massive highlight was obviously JoBerg where Atherton famously batted forever to save the match. South African fans left in disgust over this and the Barmy Army celebrated as if victory had been

achieved. I remember they were leaving, and we were chanting 'we can see you sneaking out' and 'Cheerio Cheerio!' Brilliant. In fact, the South African authorities had to ask us to leave the ground at the end because we were still celebrating. The singing went on for the whole of the last session. Athers acknowledged us – instantly becoming a Barmy Army hero. Athers didn't always smile or react to the fans – Stewey did the fan

Making up is hard to do!
New Year 1996

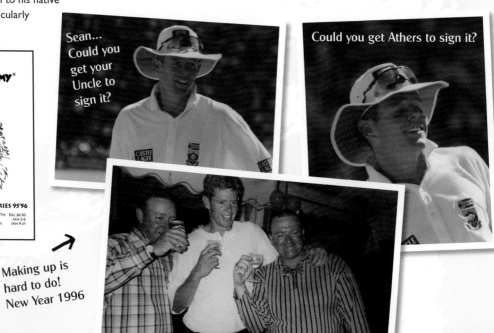

Sean... Could you get your Uncle to sign it?

Could you get Athers to sign it?

Jack Hyams president of BA Cricket Club

25 a side anyone?

Meeting the locals

BACC before the game

Chopper with sweats to give out

"Personally, however, I think that the songs come over much better through the use of our wit and humour rather than resorting to swearing."

bit for him. But with Athers it was hardly surprising as at times he almost took on teams single handed. He also had a back problem that would havedefeated most players a lot earlier in their careers.

BC: You were telling me the Sean Pollock story...

Leafy: That's Choppers story when Sean Pollock was fielding by the boundary and Chopper calls him over, and Pollock being a good sort comes over...

'Sean!'

'Yes mate?'

'If you wouldn't mind...'

Chopper hands him a bat and a pen, which Sean goes to sign until Chopper says:

'No, not you. Could you keep it and get your Uncle to sign it...?'

And then at JoBerg during Atherton's innings, Chopper calls him over again. Sean has forgotten the previous incident, so the same thing happens...

'No, not you, could you get Atherton to sign it?'

The end of this story comes ten seconds after New Year 96 when Chopper actually asks for Pollock's autograph for real and Pollock - top man - signs and has a laugh about it.

BC: What was the Barmy Army Soweto story?

Leafy: Our first cricket match under the Barmy Army CC banner was against Soweto Cricket Club on their cricket pitch in the middle of Soweto. The game was designed to give us a bit of exercise, but more importantly to raise funds for Soweto CC. This charity cricket concept has continued on all tours since then. We had a memorable

TOUR OF NEW ZEALAND 97

1st TEST AUCKLAND	24 - 28 JAN
2nd TEST WELLINGTON	6 - 10 FEB
3rd TEST CHRISTCHURCH	14 - 18 FEB
ONE DAY INTERNATIONALS	20 FEB - 4 MAR

www.barmy-army.com

day/evening and night and taught the locals some great X Certificate ditties.

BC: The next tour was New Zealand 97?

Leafy: This tour didn't generate a whole lot of new songs, to be honest But the Kiwi's loved learning the songs from the 94/5 Australia tour and have no doubt used some of them against their old adversaries since then! One good story though. We gave Chris

Cairns a bit of stick for his haircut - something along the lines of 'he's got a poodle on his head!' As a result of which he shaved it off for cancer research and the Barmy Army sold raffle ticket's at the Test and raised six thousand New Zealand dollars.

BC: West Indies 98?
Leafy: Well, its different in the West Indies. For a start they play music at the Test grounds and it tends to drown out most of the singing. Anyway, winding up West Indian bowlers is not advisable, as Curtley Ambrose proved at Sydney in the late 90's.
But, if you remember, the Jamaica Test was called off because of the state of the pitch – so we sung songs about that in the bars, but not at the grounds.

BC: Didn't Botham say 'I was fearful someone would be killed out there'?

Leafy: Yes, he did. The decision that was made was the correct one. One funny tour story though: in the nets Ashley Cowans bowled left handed and hit the stumps. David Lloyd said 'I thought you bowled right handed'. Cowans replied: "I do, but you haven't picked me as a right hander so I thought I'd try left ." We went to Trinidad after that and experienced the 'carnival' atmosphere at it's most extreme. Most song writing went on hold and it was party time both in and out of the ground. After winning the 2nd Trinidad Test the players did two laps of honour around the stadium. Then, rum-fuelled, our celebrations continued in memorable fashion outside the ground.

BC: What about player songs?
Leafy: Gus Fraser was the best bowler on that tour by a distance. He was the leading wicket taker and he had his own song which hopefully helped him to keep going in temperatures that most of us were struggling to watch cricket in, let alone play.

'My name is super Gus Fraser
I'm as sharp as a razor

I bowl right arm fast for England
England
When I walk down the street
All the people I meet
They say
Hey, big man
What's your name?
My name isSSSS'
(Lyrics, thanks to Gary Taylor)

Also Andy Caddick. To the Tune of 'My Darling Clementine'
'Andy Caddick, Andy Caddick
Must be worth 500 grand
He was too good for New Zealand
So he plays for Engerland'

There was one incident when a dog walked on to the pitch in Guyana and left an Australia shaped mound on the square, so from then on in 'Who let the Dogs out ....' was sung every night in bars all round the islands – soon to become a massive hit in the UK.

BC: Next stop. The Ashes 98/99.
Leafy: Now that's another story.

"There was one incident when a dog walked on to the pitch in Guyana and left an Australia shaped mound on the square, so from then on in 'Who let the Dogs out ....' was sung every night"

A Barbados obsession since 1884.

PRODUCT OF BARBADOS
FIVE STAR
COCKSPUR
Est'd 1884
FINE RUM

BARMY ARMY® proud sponsor of the Barmy Army Cricket Club

THE PERFECT
England Opener

Strauss is good, but wouldn't this composite player be just the ticket?

**BRAIN: Graham Gooch
(118 Tests, 1975-1995)**
Few openers organised their game as intuitively as Gooch. He found his scoring areas – off the hip, straight drive, square cut – and stuck to them. Better aged 35 than 25, Gooch developed into one of England's most reliable and inspirational players.

**BALLS: Michael Atherton
(115 Tests, 1989-2001)**
The one source of pleasure for the England fan during the great crash of the nineties was watching Michael Atherton duck, weave and wear bouncer after bouncer, day after day. If Athers was still in, we always stood a chance. Of a draw.

**DEFENCE: Geoffrey Boycott
(England, 108 Tests)**
Most blockers stonewall because they can't do much else; Sir Geoffrey blocked because, in life, he loved nothing more than watching a ball dribble impotently back up the pitch. And he was masterful. He was once dropped after scoring 246* against India, after the selectors sat through 555 minutes of agony.

**FRONT FOOT:
Sir Leonard Hutton
(79 Tests, 1937-1955)**
Yorkshire's cussed professional was a supreme front-foot player. Brought up on seaming Leeds pitches, Hutton was expert at riding the moving ball and neuter

**BACK FOOT: Alec Stewart
(133 Tests, 1990-2003)**
As with Strauss, Stewart preferred slashing cuts and knee-cocked pull shots to cover drives. Staying leg-side, he would crash anything short, and like all good back-foot players, he was rarely hit.

**FEET: Sir Jack Hobbs
(61 Tests, 1908-1930)**
The most complete opener anytime, anywhere. 198 first-class centuries, and a perfect technique to counter every style of new ball bowling. His full-stretch forward-defensive, captured in many a grainy lens, is one of cricket's grandest signifiers.

After a series of performances confirming his status as the most complete cricketer on the planet, **Andrew Flintoff** stands on the cusp of cricketing immortality. All Out Cricket's Phil Walker salutes a modern-day folk hero.

In the brief lull after Edgbaston 2005, the bloke in the street's bible ran another bombastic front page. 'FROM BEERO TO HERO' screamed The Sun, next to a photo of Andrew Flintoff, with a WORLD EXCLUSIVE (Das Bild are still seething) about how the great man won't get pissed until England have won the Ashes. Nothing more, nothing less. Now, it's not about to adorn their Wapping offices alongside GOTCHA! and IT WAS THE SUN WOT WON IT!, but in these tabloid times there can be no more articulate statement of where cricket suddenly stands.

What this told us about cricket was that a quaint old game, redolent of rain, failure and Tory heartlands, was cool again; what it said about Our Fred was that here was the icon, the movement's spokesman, on whose immense shoulders the national game could rest.

It's quite an achievement, ousting the likes of Beckham (plus missus and mistresses) and Rooney for a day, but Flintoff's ascent to the front page owes nothing to the usual smut currency, and all to that rarest modern phenomena: the acquiring of genuine excellence. You won't find any exposes with Flintoff, because there's no dirt to dish. He's married with a young daughter, and notwithstanding the earring, couldn't be further from the image of the excessive footballer – behind that diamond stud stands a character touched with both charisma and humility.

Inside the great question – could England win the Ashes – was the sub-plot of how Freddie would go. When the teams pitched up at Lord's Flintoff had played 47 Tests, but none against Australia. How good was he? Last season Richie Benaud said that many Aussies doubted him because he'd never been tested by the best. The glint in Benaud's eye suggested he knew what was coming. A quiet game with the bat at Lord's, when Warne tied him up in the second innings, was partly offset by taking Gilchrist's wicket in both innings, but the 239 run defeat told a stark story, as did Flintoff's scores of one and three. It wasn't looking good…

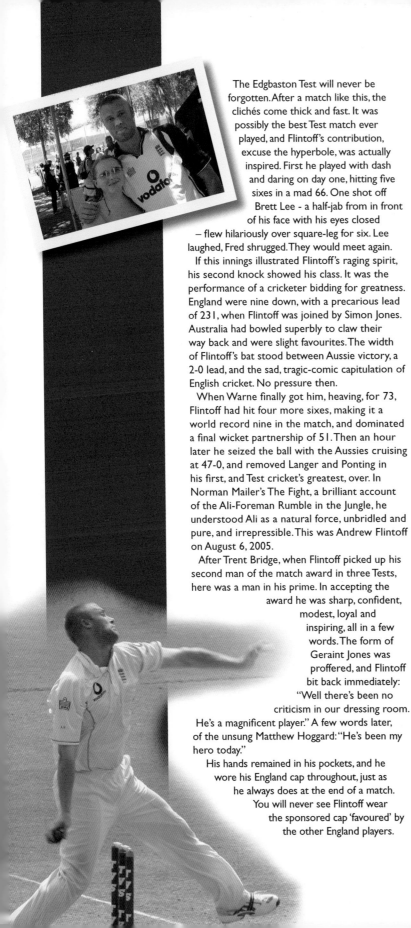

The Edgbaston Test will never be forgotten. After a match like this, the clichés come thick and fast. It was possibly the best Test match ever played, and Flintoff's contribution, excuse the hyperbole, was actually inspired. First he played with dash and daring on day one, hitting five sixes in a mad 66. One shot off Brett Lee - a half-jab from in front of his face with his eyes closed – flew hilariously over square-leg for six. Lee laughed, Fred shrugged. They would meet again.

If this innings illustrated Flintoff's raging spirit, his second knock showed his class. It was the performance of a cricketer bidding for greatness. England were nine down, with a precarious lead of 231, when Flintoff was joined by Simon Jones. Australia had bowled superbly to claw their way back and were slight favourites. The width of Flintoff's bat stood between Aussie victory, a 2-0 lead, and the sad, tragic-comic capitulation of English cricket. No pressure then.

When Warne finally got him, heaving, for 73, Flintoff had hit four more sixes, making it a world record nine in the match, and dominated a final wicket partnership of 51. Then an hour later he seized the ball with the Aussies cruising at 47-0, and removed Langer and Ponting in his first, and Test cricket's greatest, over. In Norman Mailer's The Fight, a brilliant account of the Ali-Foreman Rumble in the Jungle, he understood Ali as a natural force, unbridled and pure, and irrepressible. This was Andrew Flintoff on August 6, 2005.

After Trent Bridge, when Flintoff picked up his second man of the match award in three Tests, here was a man in his prime. In accepting the award he was sharp, confident, modest, loyal and inspiring, all in a few words. The form of Geraint Jones was proffered, and Flintoff bit back immediately: "Well there's been no criticism in our dressing room. He's a magnificent player." A few words later, of the unsung Matthew Hoggard: "He's been my hero today."

His hands remained in his pockets, and he wore his England cap throughout, just as he always does at the end of a match. You will never see Flintoff wear the sponsored cap 'favoured' by the other England players.

He seems to be saying to his supporters that the culmination of five days' graft should be honoured with the sacred cap he fought for, not the baseball hat with a phone company written all over it.

The timeline of English cricket's resurgence can be traced through Flintoff. The public's first sighting of him came in 1998 against South Africa, when he made a pair in the last match but England still won to steal the series. The BBC cameras were allowed in the dressing room for the expected raucous celebrations, yet the atmosphere made a morgue seem like Ibiza, and, as captain Alec Stewart sombrely went round shaking each player's hand, the camera panned to a bashful Flintoff, who was busy ripping down a saucy poster from behind him. Here was a boy in a man's world, and looking like he wouldn't mind getting out of it.

Which is what he did. He had a drink, put on a few pounds, and found himself a year later heavier than Lennox Lewis and struggling to get a game for Lancashire. With a career drifting badly, he was given the now famous pep-talk/ bollocking by his advisors Neil Fairbrother and 'Chubby' Chandler (gist: don't eat kebabs, have a net, be the world's best), and slowly began to push his way back.

Now contrast that scene in '98 - repressed even in victory - with the joy swelling from what Kevin Mitchell of The Observer terms 'the happiest team in sport'. Flintoff is its heartbeat, its one truly great player. He has faced the best, and smashed them out the ground - after Trent Bridge Brett Lee, another star of the summer, spoke for all his mates when professing admiration for a "supreme athlete," and a "one of a kind" cricketer.

He was consumed by this series. Eaten up by it. In the final Test Flintoff, after rescuing the batting, set to work on the Aussies. Late on Saturday he got Ponting at the beginning of a spell of 18 overs off the reel that finally finished on Sunday afternoon. He'd clearly told Vaughan not to disturb him until he'd bowled them out. In those 18 overs, on a flat pitch with the Australians looking to accelerate, he took five wickets for 38 runs. For all his great feats – the great overs, the great knocks, the great catches – this was Flintoff's finest hour. In his first Ashes series he made 402 runs (one hundred, three fifties) and took 24 wickets. The Man of the Series.

There is, of course, just one last question: how long before the pantheon of great all-rounders adds another name to the list? Miller, Sobers, Imran, Botham…Flintoff?

His time is now. ●

* "STUDYING THE CONTENTS OF THEIR STOMACHS, THEY SEEM TO SURVIVE SOLELY ON LAGER!!"

Geraint Jones
GLOVE MACHINE

It can't be easy, keeping wicket for England. For one thing, you have to spend hours on end stood next to Trescothick, Flintoff and Strauss! That's the real downside, according to stumper Geraint Jones. All Out Cricket's Jim Hindson spoke to the ever-present gloveman at the National Cricket Centre at Loughborough. All is well with the Kent man.

Loughborough University, on a soulless, bitterly cold Monday morning. Hardly what you'd call the most glamorous location for a magazine shoot...

The National Cricket Centre provides one of very few beams of light on an otherwise stark 410-acre campus. A hotchpotch of angular and largely functional buildings evoke more the feeling of cold war East Germany than middle-England seat of learning. Architecturally there is nothing that ties one faculty block to the next, aside from their collective grimness.

England's wicket-keeper shivers despite the benefit of studio lights and a proper coat. Geraint Jones cuts a handsome figure standing head bowed as he does; zipped up within his many layers. England's Papua New Guinea born, Australian reared, man of Kent is in remarkably good spirits despite leaving his Canterbury home before daybreak. This is all the more commendable considering Jones is about to undergo a day of rigorous

fitness testing at the national team's state-of-the-art base – once we've led him back from within the utilitarian maze of work space we're stuck in.

Geraint Jones is not of the smelly, 'more tweaks than a Tourette's sufferer' school of wicket-keeping. He's neatly turned out, considered in manner and actions, and on the face of things, not in the least bit mad. And with the gloves in Pakistan, despite being overshadowed with the bat by the heroics of opposite number, Kamran Akmal, he was precise, well prepared and in the same unflustered manner, it saw him give his most accomplished series performance since wearing the lions and coronet.

He made his international debut six months after the Queen welcomed the first intake to the National Academy here in November 2003. Since then, despite the odd bump in the road, he has kept in 30 consecutive Tests until he broke a finger in the second Test against Pakistan.

Jones spoke at length about the art

of keeping, Adam Gilchrist, the Ashes, and his level-headed approach to life generally. That is, of course, excluding the occasion when he was held back by team-mates as he headed for the crowd to sort out a barracker after taking the winning catch at Edgbaston – then he was steaming!

GERAINT JONES ON...
Adam Gilchrist

We did speak quite a bit after each Test. It all started back at the ICC Champions Trophy in 2004. That was the first time I played against Australia and the first chance I had to meet him. The keepers generally stick together and have a chat, but as we were both using the same kit as well it drew us together even more. I think I had some gloves that were slightly different – he was still using some older style gloves, and I had the new Puma kit. So I had one over on him!

We spoke quite a bit during last summer, and he was really good. He's got through a bit of stick as well when he first came into the side and he would say to me 'forget what they (the media) are all saying and do you best.'

'I spend so much time stood next to Tres... (pause) and I can't ignore him all day!'

At the moment, Gilly is getting quite a bit of criticism about being out of form in Australia, but he is keeping fantastically well. It is hard because when you know you are doing one aspect well, you put yourself under pressure to get the other discipline up to the same level. You put an equal amount of time in, but it does ebb and flow as to how it goes.

The State Of His Hands
Touch wood, they're ok. You get the occasional knock, but so far I've been alright. I'm sure I've broken a few fingers but I tend not to get them x-rayed! I prefer not to know what's wrong with them although they have gone a few funny shapes.

I don't tape any fingers – I don't like the feeling. I've seen some keepers who have every finger tape, but it feels a bit funny, and I'm usually late in the morning so time is an issue!

The England Slip Cordon
I generally like to listen to Fred giving Tres (Marcus Trescothick) some stick. And then we have to cope with the boring pair of Andrew Strauss and Tres talking about their cars. You have to find ways of getting through the day. I spend so much time stood next to Tres…(pause) and I can't ignore him all day!

Mannerisms
You see someone like Karl Krikken and what he used to do. And the mad badger Paul Nixon, he was forever stretching. I watched him go through those mannerisms at Kent for three years, so perhaps that's rubbed off on me – as in, I try to be as normal as possible! I guess you are not so aware of your own tweaks, but I don't think I have that many.

I do like my inner gloves to be dry though. I also don't like the smell of used keepers inners and if Jen (Jones' partner) can smell my hands before I come through the door she'll have a go at me!

Coping In The Media Spotlight
Generally it's through making a mistake that you get the tough times. So I just try to analyse that mistake and work out how and why it went wrong and address it. Once I've done that I'm happy to discard it! Relatively happy anyway. It's just the papers over the next day where it keeps coming up. Generally, I'll work out what happened quickly – you know straight away what you've done wrong. I've got used to learning from

Photo: All Out Cricket

mistakes and getting over them.

I think because of those low times, if I do well, I don't want to be over the top. You'd be heading for a fall, just try to be quite constant. Someone like Michael Vaughan is incredible for that, he's on a constant level all the time. So I've watched and tried to learn from that, and no matter how I perform, just be the same person.

Planning A Wedding
I'm supposed to be getting married in September, so the honeymoon is going to be tough to sort. The way the schedule looks at the moment she might just about get a night away in London! It is tough – and possibly the hardest thing about playing. You have so little time and it's also difficult to look ahead, because I never even pencil my name in, expecting to play in future series. I guess the longer you spend in the side, the better you have to get at organising your private life.

Keeping On The Sub-Continent
The ball comes through low, with the pitches being slower. And you have to stand closer to take the ball on the full. There's not too much up around head height and you have to be concentrating and aware that everything is coming through at knee and hip height.

It's something I worked on before I went away, in here (points to the National Cricket Centre building) and when I was out there as well. It helped a lot – just to tell the brain its skidding lower and then react to it.

I didn't try to change too much for India. I like to keep the same routine. Once I have done that routine, then it's a case of where my focus is. In Pakistan and India I spent a lot of time with the spinners before the day started, because they would be doing te majority of the bowling. Whereas somewhere like Australia, it will be a case of taking more balls from the seamers. My general routine stays the same, it's just what I work on after the routine, before play starts, where the variation comes in.

The Keepers' Union
I remember Alec Stewart saying to the India keeper, Parthiv Patel, that he wouldn't have a chat about keeping until the end of the series. Maybe that's a philosophy to take on board because you don't really want any member of the opposition to get a break. Brad Haddin, the Australia back up wicket-keeper, had a chat with me about how to cope on tour when you are not playing. I'd been on a few tours when Chris Read was keeping, so that came up in conversation and that's more touring life than coping with foreign conditions.

Sledging
It's more a general banter with the guys around. I don't feel the need to go at the opposition batsmen too much because you can create something that backfires on you. If I have a go at every single one of them, there is going to be eleven of them against me when I go out there. I keep it to my team, but if there's a need for it, I will say something. We had that in Pakistan during the one-dayers when their batsmen were coming out to bat before Shahid Afridi, and all the crowd wanted was to see him. So we had a bit of fun with that.

Generally, once the ball has been delivered, we switch off quite well and have a chat to one another. So the opposition batsmen probably do feel quite isolated - and it's a good thing to have against them. We don't want to engage with the opposition and make them too comfortable. If you do end up chatting with them, it can put them at ease and you wouldn't want to do that.

Has The Ashes Changed Your Life?
Yes – a little bit. In terms of recognition, and obviously the MBE was a fantastic award. I haven't been to university, so it's great to have some letters after my name! So many people watched and were captivated by the series and there is still a lot of goodwill out there. It's nice that people still congratulate you when you are out and about.

Jumping Into The Crowd At Edgbaston
If the guys hadn't got hold of me, yeah, I think I would have been over the boards – I was a bit pumped up! When we got into the dressing room after, the guys who were holding me back said they didn't realise the strength that I pack. I'm quite thankful – I could have done a Cantona! I had been getting a bit of stick, and it was one of those moments in a game where something just happens. I'm glad I did it. ●

GOING ON TOUR:
The Essential Barmy Army Guide To Touring
3. make sure you have liquid refreshment as some places on the planet don't!

CRICKET'S MOSTACHIOSO

Moustaches. The Love Slug, Pencil Line and full-on Magnum PI's are all given due consideration as we count down the top 10 top lips.

10 CRAIG MCMILLAN

Full Name: Craig Douglas McMillan
Born: September 13 1976, Christchurch, Canterbury
Major Teams: Canterbury, Gloucestershire & New Zealand
Played: 1994- present day
Moustache Type: Post-modern ironic handlebar

With nothing much to do on New Zealand's 2003/4 tour to Bangladesh, Craig McMillan put together this bad boy of a look for your consideration. Always a man with a very personal sense of style, 'Macca' managed to perfectly capture (in bristles) what it means to many players to be away on tour. The phrase 'one for the boys' comes to mind.

9 JAVED MIANDAD

Full Name: Mohammad Javed Miandad Khan
Born: June 12 1957, Karachi, Sind
Major Teams: Karachi Cricket Association, Sind, Sussex, Habib Bank Limited, Glamorgan & Pakistan
Played: 973-1994
Moustache Type: Schoolboy's back pocket hair comb meets Velcro fastening

A notoriously committed competitor, Javed Miandad was never far from controversy. At Perth in 1983/84 he raised the bar of bad behaviour to new heights when hoisting his bat to strike Australia's Dennis Lillee, only to be separated by umpire Tony Crafter.

Apparently, Lillee felt his own moustache had more lustre than Javed's, and he told him so. Javed was not happy and replied that Lillee's looked as if it were dyed. Yadda, yadda, yadda. One thing leads to another and eventually World War III breaks out.

A bit of advice for you - don't disrespect the mo'. Don't even go there, it's not a pleasant place and it just isn't worth it.

8 RICHARD ILLINGWORTH

Full Name: Richard Keith Illingworth
Born: August 23 1963, Greengates, Bradford, Yorkshire
Major Teams: Worcestershire, Natal, Derbyshire & England
Played: 1982-2001
Moustache Type: Teenage bum fluff infused with more than just a hint of Only Fools and Horses' Mickey Pearce

Yorkshire born slow left armer Richard Illingworth played nine Tests between 1991 and 1996, sporting a moustache throughout. Illingworth ploughed a lone furrow in an era that was almost totally devoid of lip furniture. And good on him for trying!

The moustache was not related to former England coach and chairman of selectors, Raymond Illingworth.

7 'CATERPILLAR' KAPIL DEV

Full Name: Kapil Dev Ramlal Nikhanj
Born: January 6 1959, Chandigarh, India
Major Teams: Haryana (India), Northamptonshire, Wocestershire & India
Played: 1975-1995
Moustache Type: Love Slug

In his pomp this inky-haired troubadour of an allrounder represented the 'ying' to Imran Khan's 'yang' creating the living embodiment of Asian cricket's love alliance. Tall. Swarthy. A dapper dresser, blessed with cow-like eyelashes. You just name me a woman that wouldn't want to worship at this love god's temple.

6 RICE & HADLEE

Full Name: Clive Edward Butler Rice
Born: July 23 1949, Johannesburg, Transvaal
Major Teams: Transvaal, Nottinghamshire, Natal, Scotland & South Africa
Played: 1969-1994
Moustache Type: Magnum PI leaning towards Hulk Hogan

Full Name: (Sir) Richard John Hadlee
Born: July 3 1951, St Albans, Christchurch, Canterbury
Major Teams: Canterbury, Nottinghamshire, Tasmania & New Zealand
Played: 1970-1990
Moustache Type: World War II spiv

You get two for the price of one with these titans of eighties cricket. Hadlee, Sir Richard to you, and Rice, just Clive, both bestrode the county game like twin towers Hadlee being the only man to win the PCA Player of the Year Award on three different occasions; Rice captaining South Africa in its first games back after re-admission to world cricket in 1991.

Both world-class allrounders, both sartorially challenged.

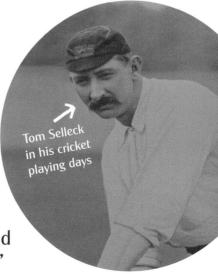

Tom Selleck in his cricket playing days

"Lillee felt his own moustache had more lustre than Javed's... Javed was not happy and replied that Lillee's looked as if it were dyed."

GUCCI

Full Name: Graham Alan Gooch
Born: July 23 1953, Whipps Cross, Leytonstone, Essex
Major Teams: Essex, Western Province & England
Played: 1973-2000
Moustache Type: Christmas cracker clip-on meets western gunslinger

This Essex man first pitched up for England with his souped-up, blacked-out and furry-dice adorned hirsuteness in 1975. And pretty well from that year on, him and 'it' were synonymous with the few batting successes that came England's way in the eighties and nineties.

What a career – nearly 9,000 Test runs, 44,000 first-class runs, 22,000 limited over runs, 581 first-class appearances, 128 first-class hundreds – and most of them accompanied by his Mexican bandit bigote.

Graham Gooch – one man and his mo' went to mow a bowler (or two, or three).

DAVID 'BUTCHY THE DOG-FACE BOY' BOON

Full Name: David Clarence Boon
Born: December 29 1960, Launceston, Tasmania
Major Teams: Tasmania, Durham & Australia
Played: 1978-1999
Moustache Type: Walrus

If Boon had played in any era other than the one lorded over by 'Big Merv' his facial forestation would have set him apart. Despite working his socks off with his overhanging, bushy and otherwise unruly mo', Boon always looked like a smaller inner layer of a Mervyn Hughes, Russian babushka doll. Bless.

DK

Full Name: Dennis Keith Lillee
Born: July 18 1949, Subiaco, Perth, Western Australia
Major Teams: Western Australia, Tasmania, Northamptonshire & Australia
Played: 1969-1988

Moustache Type: Straight up, no messing Love Slug

In the he-man heyday of 1970s Australia, Dennis Lillee was the living breathing embodiment of sex-on-legs. The type of man who needed to make sure he went everywhere with a 'shitty stick' in order to keep the crumpet off.

And it was the luxuriant top-lipped 'pout pelt' that helped put him there. Shirt open to the waist, chest hair freshly mown and combed, Lillee was seventies cricket's definitive medallion man.

Forget all notions of 'caught Marsh, bowled Lillee' – just smell that Hai Karate!

RICHIE RICHARDSON

Full Name: Richard Benjamin Richardson
Born: January 12 1962, Five Islands Village, Antigua
Played: 1981-1997
Major Teams: Leeward Islands, Yorkshire, Northern Transvaal, Windward Islands & West Indies
Moustache Type: Pencil Line with Love Slug undertones

Batting throughout his career without a helmet and with only his lip fur for protection, Richardson looked a man who could hook yorkers let alone bouncers for six. A definitive Caribbean bladesman in spirit and style and as captain of the Windies, Richie Richardson epitomised cool. The classic West Indies mo'man.

"The type of man who needed to make sure he went everywhere with a 'shitty stick' in order to keep the crumpet off. And it was the luxuriant top-lipped 'pout pelt' that helped put him there."

'SWERVIN' MERVYN HUGHES

Full Name: Mervyn Gregory Hughes
Born: November 23 1961, Euroa, Victoria
Major Teams: Victoria, Essex, Australian Capital Territory & Australia
Played: 1981-1995
Moustache Type: Uber-Magnum PI with hoochie tendencies

Viewed by many as one of the founding fathers of the great Australian side of recent times, Merv Hughes was a favourite wherever he went. An obvious tryer. And a figure who further endeared himself to supporters with his ungainly run to the wicket (reminiscent of a shopping trolley on a cobbled street), his sloshing waistline and his confrontational on-field manner.

But let's be right about this, it was the Sydney-style 'leather boy' moustache that tipped the fans over the edge.

And again, let's be right. It looked absolutely bloody stupid!

BEEFY

Full Name: Ian Terence Botham
Born: November 24 1955, Oldfield, Heswall, Cheshire
Major Teams: Somerset, Worcestershire, Queensland, Durham & England
Played: 1974-1993
Moustache Type: Fox meets hair

Back in the late seventies and on through the eighties, there were few things that England cricket fans could rely on.

One thing was that the national side would be annihilated by the West Indies losing by a 'whatever to nil' score line. Whilst amid that torture and turmoil, England would pick 36 different cricketers to wear the lions and coronet, of which 9 of them would have a go at being captain, 14 would retire hurt never to be seen again, and one man would appear out of the smoking wreckage with reputation dented, but in tact. A reputation and level of performance that would then go through the roof whenever the next series' opponents were Australia.

As good, bad or indifferent as his team mates were, Botham became 'Beefy' when facing the old enemy. Without Botham there would be no Ashes as we know it. Without Botham's moustache, the images from those hazy, lazy days would not be what they are. And without those images, we would hardly be able to remember if we did ever actually beat the ockers.

As a 'tache - for me it was a bit of a disappointment. But if asked if Ian Terence Botham is this country's greatest living Englishman? There has to be only one answer and that answer begins with a well pressed uniform, a click of the heels, a shoulders back and a smart salute. And it finishes with a wholeheartedly bellowed: "YES, SIR! YES, SIR! I SHOULD JOLLY WELL COCOA!"

TRIMMED!

A couple that just missed the cut, as it were...

1ST RESERVE. GARTH LE ROUX

Full Name: GARTH STERLING LE ROUX
Born: September 4 1955, Kenilworth, Cape Town, Cape Province, South Africa
Major Teams: Western Province & Sussex
Played: 1975-1989
Moustache Type: Tarzan

A South African cricketer who's career spanned the apartheid era. Fearsome fast bowler who formed part of a superb new ball attack with Imran Khan during the pair's careers at Sussex. Huge competitor who was by all accounts as gentle as a lamb off the field. Aren't they all...

2ND RESERVE: MURRAY 'MUZZA' BENNETT

Full Name: MURRAY JOHN BENNETT
Born: October 6 1956, Brisbane, Queensland
Major Teams: New South Wales & Australia
Played: 1982-1988
Moustache Type: Droopy beer catcher

Toured England with Allan Border's 1995 Australians and was panned everywhere. Bennett, not content with just a ridiculous mo', went one step further by adding appalling 'prescription' sunglasses to enhance the look.

Taken from All Out Cricket magazine, available from WHSmith or subscribe at www.alloutcricket.co.uk

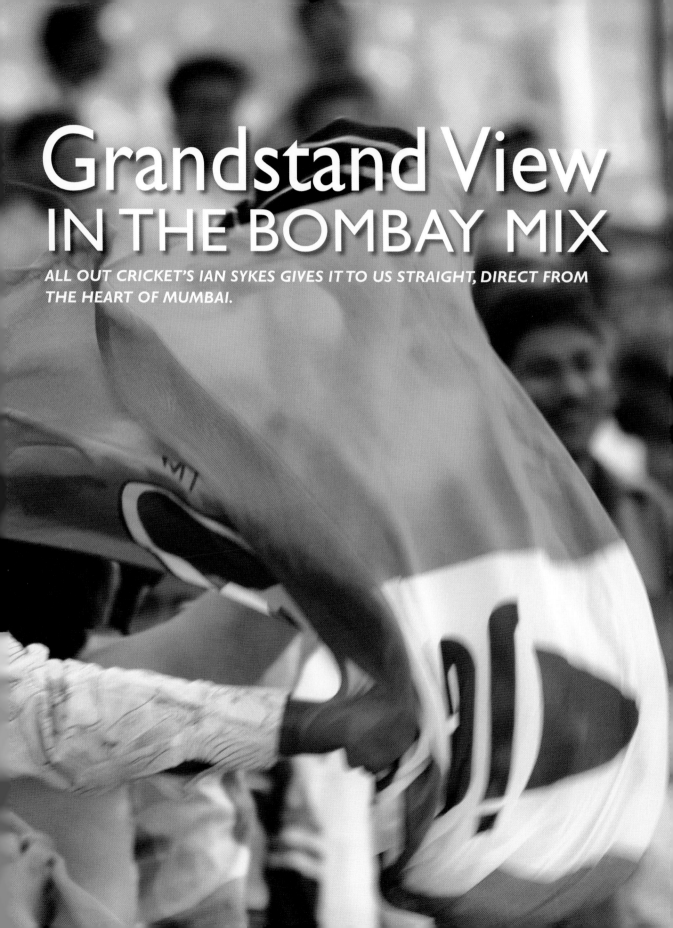

Grandstand View
IN THE BOMBAY MIX

ALL OUT CRICKET'S IAN SYKES GIVES IT TO US STRAIGHT, DIRECT FROM THE HEART OF MUMBAI.

Not in my wildest dreams did I imagine that Flintoff and his England 'A' side would level the series as I settled down to watch the first day's play in Mumbai.

Inside the last 12 months, I've been to Istanbul to see Liverpool win their fifth European Championship, I've seen England's cricket team regain the Ashes for the first time in almost 20 years at The Oval, and now I've seen Andrew Flintoff's depleted team become the first England side to win a Test match in India since David Gower's boys back in 1985. Perhaps somebody would like to buy me tickets to follow Sven's England in Germany?

Only during the time between Hernan Crespo scoring AC Milan's third goal and Steven Gerrard scoring Liverpool's first did I really doubt that the Reds could win in Istanbul, and I always knew that England would regain the Ashes. I even put £50 on Vaughan's men after the Lord's Test (£50 of Betfair's money…note where Mr Sykes originates – Ed). But not in my wildest dreams did I imagine that Flintoff and his England 'A' side would level the series as I settled down to watch the first day's play in Mumbai.

It wasn't the fact that they were coming off the back of a sound defeat in Chandigarh. Nor was it because the squad was weary, and

decimated by injury and illness. The most daunting factor facing that side in Mumbai was the Wankhede Stadium. The Wankhede is far removed from what we in England consider a Test match ground – Jonathan Agnew apparently suggested on Test Match Special that it was one of the few grounds in world cricket that managed to live up to its name. It feels unfinished, smells of open sewers and I can't imagine there being a space anywhere within its walls where it's possible to get comfortable for five minutes. Most daunting, it is inhabited by the most partisan crowd I have ever experienced. It's not a place for the vulnerable to come good, and England were vulnerable.

At various stages during the Ashes last summer, the English crowds lifted Vaughan's men. Likewise after the Champions League Final, the Liverpool players lauded the travelling Reds, who were so vocal throughout that night in May. Singing "We're going to win 4-3" may have been a tad optimistic at half time, but when Andriy Shevchenko stepped up to take Milan's fifth penalty in the shoot-out,

there was no way the poor guy was going to score it. The Liverpool supporters ruined him.

In Mumbai it was England who were subjected to torrents of pressure by the Indian fans. Sitting in the Wankhede Stadium, I was a minority supporter, not something I'm used to. Every time the ball passed the bat of Strauss or Bell on that first morning, the crowd erupted as if the match was won. I thought this was just a bit of frenzied Day One energy that would be burned off by the Mumbai sun by lunchtime, but they never relented. The noise was deafening, all day, singing, chanting and doing that ever-annoying

Mexican wave. The Barmy Army was in the minority, and whenever old Jimmy got up with his flag and his one song, Mumbai drowned him out.

As the Test went on, the local fans upped their game, and perhaps pushed the banter beyond what we would call cricket. Any Englishman fielding on the perimeter was greeted with "Asshole, Asshole…" and Matthew Hoggard's work rate was acknowledged with chants of: "Wey-oh, wey-oh, Hoggy is a donkey." Perhaps worst of all was the chant directed at our skipper, suggesting that he might be partial to a bit of self-pleasure. Each day at the Wankhede was a test of England's mettle. Every time they seemed to falter, the crowd smelt blood. In the past, this was the point at which England would self-destruct, but not this time. Flintoff, Hoggard and co regrouped constantly, digging deep into their reserves and coming back to every heckle with a smart one-liner.

England's resilience throughout the Test was encapsulated by Monty Panesar on Day Five, when he lost that regulation catch after an irresponsible shot from Indian hero Mahendra Singh Dhoni, and ran about in circles for a while before eventually appearing to field the ball by hearing alone. The Indian crowd loved this and went to town on the English youngster with whistles, jibes and catcalls. A couple of balls later and Dhoni played exactly the same shot. Poor Monty wasn't getting away from this, and could easily have gone all Shevchenko, but he held his nerve and took the catch. For the first time in five days, the Mumbai crowd went silent. It was a silence that meant more to the fielding side than any ovation the overwhelmed England supporters could muster up all week.

Hoggard's work rate was acknowledged with chants of: "Wey-oh, wey-oh, Hoggy is a donkey."

TOP TEN

Run ups

When looking at any great bowler the first thing to study is the run-up. The run-up is underestimated in its value by casual observers, but any bowler will tell you that a lost run-up means a bowler lost. We've seen some crackers, some funny and some just plain odd.

ANDREW CADDICK
The Straight-Legged Mincing Mimic

10 What a bowler was Caddick. You've gotta love him. Up there with England's finest bowlers of modern times, and with a run-up modelled to an almost comical degree on his hero Richard Hadlee. It would start, then stop, then he'd look to run, then he'd stop again, then he'd straighten his leg like it's snapping backwards, and then finally, just when you thought it was all over, he'd start running again. Size 48 feet added to the comedy, and with a Tourettes-style bowling hand pointedly, uncontrollably flaring out from his right side, the batsman often didn't know whether to laugh or defend.

"It was said umpires could not hear him running in, and batsmen looked elsewhere to avoid being hypnotized into stasis"

MICHAEL HOLDING
Whispering Death

9 If Holding were an animal he'd be that lizard that runs on water, his feet silently kissing the surface en route to its prey. The grace of his approach – head regally cocked as those long legs ate up the parched turf – was at odds with the violence erupting from delivery. It was said umpires could not hear him running in, and batsmen looked elsewhere to avoid being hypnotized into stasis. Observers and batsmen alike would scratch their heads and wonder how something so beautiful could be so devastating.

WAQAR YOUNIS
The 50-yard Dasher

8 There's nothing quite as intimidating as a tearaway quick that uses the sightscreen to push off for the start of his run. The textbook run-up is one that builds in momentum as the bowler approaches the crease. The Younis run-up is like the 50-yard sprint: he starts off sprinting, sprints in the middle, and sprints at the end only to slow a little when he suddenly flips his legs round, jumps into a huge delivery stride, and hurls a 90mph inswinging yorker. Yet with Waqar there was never any hint he was out of control. He had perfect balance and great rhythm, not to mention stamina, but the key to it all was intimidation, and the idea that if the ground was any bigger then so would his run-up.

CURTLY AMBROSE
The Antiguan Spaceman

At 6ft 7in, the gentle giant from the Leewards strode to the bowling crease, his knees kicking skywards as if his feet are being scalded by the burning turf, and those white sweatbands glistening with menace. In a perfect world NASA would have been an Antiguan invention, Curtly would have been Neil Armstrong, and 'one small step for man, one huge step for mankind' would have held more relevance. Every one of his 405 test wickets was greeted by his mum ringing a bell outside her Antiguan home to alert the locals that Curtly had struck; either that or to alert low flying aircraft to pull up their landing wheels as those sweatbands punched the air in celebration.

DEREK PRINGLE
The Rocking Nodding Horse Dog.

Suggs was always known as the rocking horse. First he looks up at the batsman shyly, pleading for a bit of compassion, like a nodding dog. Then the head goes forward as if to force the feet to follow, and then rocking the head back like suddenly going uphill. This repeats itself until the bowler reaches his delivery stride. Possible advantage – gives sense of rhythm. Definite disadvantage – looks ridiculous. And the pace was always a bit wavy, as if he secretly wanted to be a spinner. By the time the arm turned over, he may as well have been.

ANDREW FLINTOFF
The Quentin Crisp

When he jumps into delivery, you don't want to be at the other end. He's a big unit and uses every ounce of it. But what's all that in the middle? Those little mincing steps like he's blundered halfway through his run and can't get to the loo? This is Flintoff, everything should be big; instead he pussyfoots around like a 6ft 4in Wayne Sleep impersonator. Soon they stretch out again, and the true figure bears down from what's eventually a well-structured run, but for a few moments you do wonder…

> If Holding's approach is mesmerising, then Warne's is enquiring, it's like he's asking: "Why don't you hit me? I'm only walking."

Cricket: Make your body strong & save your kids from evil society!! →

BOB DYLAN WILLIS
The Brazilian

So called because he'd go off on a barely credible tangent, where after starting towards the batsman, he then veers off to the side towards extra-cover puffing and panting and letting his arm work like an oar behind his back. You think he might be trying to turn around and start again, but then he starts back towards the crease, desperately trying to get there without missing it altogether and careering into mid-off. Watch Rivelino strike a left-foot free-kick in 1970, and you'll know where we are.

PHIL EDMONDS
The Stubborn Southpaw

The yips. Every spinner's nightmare. It's a Test match in the early Eighties, and England left-armer Phil Edmonds is suffering. But Edmonds wasn't the sort to take this lying down, so in place of a smooth, rhythmical action, he marched, Gestapo style, to the crease. He just marched. When he got there he was able to let go of the bloody thing, and somehow get it down the other end. It was odd, sad, but strangely heroic. And this is the best bit; he bowled alright. Always a cantankerous old bugger, was Edmonds, stubborn and independent-minded; the yips devil couldn't have chosen a worse bloke to go after.

HARBHAJAN SINGH
The Pogo

What a run-up. All windmilling arms and structured chaos. He comes in at a 45-degree angle, ripping the ball manically from hand to hand, bouncing along like a pogo obsessive at a farmhouse rave. When he gets to the crease he throws his kicking legs wildly sideways, and we're back in the disused barn at 5am – before bounding into delivery. After that, the rest takes care of itself.

SHANE WARNE
The Walking Wizard

No cricket top ten is complete without Warne. The round Victorian with a taste for floozies, fame and flippers. The greatest player of the modern age and the best leggie of all time. He stands, spins the ball from one hand to the other, fixes his glare on the batsman and then walks into his delivery stride before a sudden burst of electricity, and the revolving grenade is off on its wicked way. If Holding's approach is mesmerising, then Warne's is enquiring, it's like he's asking: "Why don't you hit me? I'm only walking."

Drinks break

At the professional level of cricket, everyone recognises the drinks break as a couple of minutes in the middle of a session for players take on fluids, or for spectators to go for a walk to relieve themselves of the same. By Andrew Tingey

At the amateur level things are basically quite similar. However several years ago my club had a match where one of our players had a very different interpretation of what was meant by "drinks".

We were playing in a bottom-of-the-table clash. A six-pointer in "football-ese". My team batted first and things were not going well. The opposition's umpire was evidently umpiring for his club, and some very strange decisions were being given.

Our hugely-talented-but-psychologically-damaged top-order batsman, let's call him Tim, had got himself in, only to be curiously given out LBW, well forward, outside the line, etc, etc. Poor Tim was beside himself. Several more wickets went down: batsmen were caught behind off the boot, more LBW's with plenty of bat involved, a dubious run-out, etc.

As we watched the carnage from the boundary's edge Tim said he really fancied a drink of milk, and asked if anyone wanted anything from the local shop as he was just off to get some stuff.

Tim returned with shopping bags clanking away. Milk, sweets, newspapers, chocolate, etc. And, as we later found out, a bottle of vodka in brown paper bag.

At tea we had been triggered for little more 140, with no less than six shockingly bad umpiring decisions. We rallied ourselves over the egg sarnies and bakewell tarts. We should be able to do this...

Tim was highly animated in the field, exhorting us to greater efforts. He did, however, seem to be having difficulty catching the ball as it was relayed back to the bowlers, hands flapping madly, a crazed look on his face.

It was only a matter of time before the oppo's umpire scored his seventh. A massive edge, caught behind, from their top-scorer and eventual match winner, was given not out. This was too much for Tim, who, it suddenly dawned upon us was by now paralytic. Tim staggered, circling round towards the umpire, and began, I suppose, to verbally abuse him. No-one could understand what he was saying, but the umpire was having none of it. As captain I escorted Tim to the relative safety of the outfield.

Eventually I decided that even deep backward square was not safe for him, so I thanked him for his efforts, and got him to the dressing room.

We lost that match, and subsequently we had to empty some of Tim's personal refreshment down the sink at a couple matches soon after. But happily Tim went on to win his own battle, and is still hugely-talented, but now a less psychologically-damaged top-order batsman.

Postscript. I really did not want to meet up with that umpire ever again. However the following spring, on tour in Christchurch, New Zealand, taking a quiet stroll round the Botanic Gardens the day before the First Test, who should appear around the corner? My companions looked on in amusement as I dashed up a side path. You could not make it up!

CANTOR
spreadfair

An alternative explanation of Spread Betting

You're at the cricket. It's hot, so inevitably you need plenty of liquid refreshment throughout the day.

A few beers, plenty of sunshine, and a few more beers is the recipe for a bladder testing day. Cantor Spreadfair predicts that during a day at the cricket, the average fan will need to visit the Gents about 4-5 times.

Just like Bruce's 'Play your Cards Right', you bet higher or lower (you bet higher at the high price or lower at the low price).

If you think less than 4 visits to the WC, SELL at 4 for £1 a pee (you then win £1 for every pee you fall short of 4 and lose £1 for every pee above 4).
If you think more than 5 calls of nature, BUY at 5 for £1 a pee (you then win £1 for every pee above 5 and lose £1 for every pee you fall short of 5)

You've just had a spread bet.

For more information about a sports spread betting account with Cantor Spreadfair, log on to www.cantorspreadfair.com or call 08000 111 441, quoting 'Barmy Army'.

Spread betting is a leveraged product that can rapidly result in losses substantially in excess of your initial stake. Ensure you understand the risks as it may not be suitable for everyone.

Cantor Spreadfair is a division of Cantor Index. Cantor Index is authorised and regulated by the Financial Services Authority.

cantorspreadfair.com   08000 111 441

RAW POWER

WITH THE EMERGENCE OF KP, ENGLAND HAVE TWO MEN CAPABLE OF ACTS OF EXTREME CRICKETING VIOLENCE. BUT WHO ELSE IS UP THERE IN TERMS OF THEIR CAPACITY FOR DAMAGE?

CHRIS CAIRNS

(New Zealand)

Style: Right-handed all-rounder that hits straight and hard.

Forte: A destroyer of orthodox finger spinners.

Pet Shot: Lofted off/on drive when running down the wicket to the spinner

Achilles Heel: Extreme pace and mystery spinner.

Capacity for Mayhem: ***

The Match: ICC Trophy final NZ v India, 2000 – scored unbeaten hundred (102*) to win his country's first major cricketing trophy.

Summary: Maybe two or three years ago, the immensely strong Kiwi would have found himself at the top of the pile. But of late, a lack of match action and only mixed success means Cairns finds himself up there, but not at the top of our ranking. When on song, no run rate is out of his compass. Has tempered his game in recent times as a concession to match situations and the passing of time. Still someone that any opposition knows they have to get out – and quickly.

Andrew Flintoff

(England)

Style: Right-handed all-rounder that drives the ball to distraction.

Forte: Medium pacers beware

Pet Shot: Punched drive over mid-off facing the seamer

Achilles Heel: Can hole out in the deep when unsure of the best approach to a run chase.

Capacity for Mayhem: ***1/2

The Match: England v West Indies at Edgbaston, 2004 – scored 167 and was dropped by his dad, Colin, 'fielding' in the top tier of the Eric Hollies Stand.

Summary: Still the people's champion. When Flintoff walks to the wicket, everything is still possible for England.

Kevin Pietersen
(England)
Style: Right-handed batsman that manipulates the ball to leg, as well as beating the living daylights out of it.
Forte: The best end of innings hitter in the world today.
Pet Shot: Cow shot off seamer
Achilles Heel: Can be caught cold when first at the wicket. Susceptible to LBW shouts when faced with the swinging white ball.

Chris Gayle
(West Indies)
Style: Left-handed opener. The trickiest spinner in one-day cricket
Forte: Natural striker of the ball. Hits short of a length balls through the off-side as if facing a throw down.
Pet Shot: Back foot drive against the new ball
Achilles Heel: Quality, short of a length, seam bowler taking the ball away from him. Can also lack confidence and the precise footwork that goes with it.
Capacity for Mayhem: ****
The Match: South Africa v West Indies at Cape Town, 2004. A 79-ball hundred (116), made in 90 minutes, 86 of the runs (20 fours and a six) in boundaries.
Summary: On song, you simply can't bowl at the tall Jamaican. Pitch up and he'll hit the ball over mid-off, bowl short of a length and he'll slice you through the off-side. When really going Gayle makes you wonder why everyone doesn't play like him. Off colour… you understand why.

Capacity for Mayhem: ****
The Match: England v Australia ODI at Bristol, 2005. Match-winning 91* — Ask Jason Gillespie and Michael Kasprowicz what they thought of this innings…
Summary: England's biggest success story of 2005. Can knock the ball around for singles or clear even the biggest of boundaries, what price on KP leading England to World Cup success in West Indies, 2007?

Adam Gilchrist
(Australia)
Style: Left-handed keeper/batsman who opens the innings in one-day cricket and can have the match sewn up in the first 15 overs.
Forte: Picks the ball up on length, depositing it over midwicket. When eye is in, no ground looks big enough.
Pet Shot: Cuts like Zorro
Achilles Heel: Can nick out early on, especially if the ball is moving away from him in the air.
Capacity for Mayhem: *****
The Match: South Africa v Australia at Johannesburg, 2002. 204* with eight towering sixes and 19 fours, played during at turbo-charged first Test at the Wanderers.
Summary: Always scores at a run-a-ball, in Tests or ODIs. Can hit anything anywhere and such is his eye, it looks inevitable when doing so. Holds the bat like a prep school opening batsman and hits the ball like a tennis pro — possesses the best forehand cross-court in cricket.

What do you think? Have we missed anyone off the list – have your say by emailing us at comments@alloutcricket.co.uk

ARMY MANOUEVRES

By Andrew Tingey

New Zealand 2002

One of my most poignant memories was watching England at the Basin Reserve, Wellington in 2002. The rain had wrecked the match as a serious contest, and the only item of note on the field was watching Freddie continue to bed himself into the Test side with a buccaneer 75 in the second innings. There was none of the excitement of Christchurch the previous week: double-hundreds from Astle and Thorpe, and Fred's maiden Test century. We amused ourselves listening to the Barmy Army decry: "You've got the worst scoreboard in the world". It was rather like a fridge which had run out of alphabetic magnets. For example, CAddICK, with two inverted "P"s.

The Beige Brigade drank beer on their couches in the drizzle, as one English lad chanted "Barmy Army" continuously for an hour and a half, with his trousers round his ankles, resplendent in Union Jack shorts, pumping his umbrella up and down to the beat.

But the worst was the hushed whispers that spread around the quiet ground as those with radio headphones passed on Aggers' news that Ben Hollioake had died in a car accident. The minute's silence at the start of the next session was duly observed by everyone in the ground, and with the tears of the Surrey lads, Butch, Thorpey and Ramps.

> "You've got the worst scoreboard in the world".

TRINIDAD 2004

At the other end of the scale was Trinidad 2004:

It was a tough choice: an extra £20 per day to sit in the Trini Posse ? Unlimited free beer, cocktails, lunch, tea, and The Carib Girls ? Where do we sign-up ?

Not too many shouts of "Siiiddddddoooooowwwwnnn !!"

Steve Harmison and Simon Jones blew the Windies away, and the music blasted out from the Trini Posse Stand. We had two fat local ladies fighting over their man (while he was trying to make a quiet escape), some game English girls joined in the "wining" contest, and when Mick Jagger was spotted by our DJ far above us in the next stand, some massed Jumpin' Jack FlashDancing, everyone pouting and clapping. Mick gave us a friendly wave, but sadly didn't come down to join in. Dean Headley did though !

Butch guided England to victory. He had curiously spent most of his time in the field in front of the Carib Girls. At the end of the match Gareth Batty and Paul Collingwood came over to take photos of the crowd. Isn't it supposed to be the other way around ?

Fantastic road trip to the north coast of Trinidad the next day: beautiful beaches, some locals whacking the head of some weird kind of sea-eel, a return through the incredibly noisy rain forest. We had an early start the following morning to fly home. Coach will leave at 6.30am for the airport, they said. We entered a deserted hotel reception at 6.28, just in time to see the dust settle and listen to several fading gear changes. Thanks for hanging on for us, guys ! Amazingly Katy Cooke appeared from somewhere. Nothing to do with our tour party, she very kindly organised a taxi. Cheers !

SOUTH AFRICA 2005

Test Cricket — **Test Cricket**

18:02

CAN THE OWNER
OF A SILVER BMW
NTY 766 GP
PLEASE REMOVE YOUR
CAR ITS
BLOCKING THE
ENGLISH TEAMS' BUS

TOTAL 24 I

Congratulations
South Africa

...IS MOTOR COMPANY

England could not
get away from
Centurion fast enough...

Not only did we get stuffed in
the one-dayers (only KP showed
up), but to add insult to injury,
England could not get away from
Centurion fast enough...

England player Q&A's

GARETH BATTY

**IN AND AROUND THE
ENGLAND SQUAD
WHO IS THE:**

Funniest	Robert Key
Coolest	Me
Untidiest	Andrew Flintoff
Most mature	Marcus Trescothick
Wisest	Andrew Strauss
Trendiest	James Anderson
Organised	Marcus Trescothick
Most uncouth	Andrew Flintoff
Best at some thing else	Marcus Trescothick – Eating
Smoothest	Mark Butcher
Brightest	Paul Collingwood
Tightest	Geraint Jones
Most qualified	Andrew Strauss
Cricket thinker	Andrew Strauss

GOING ON TOUR:
The Essential Barmy Army Guide To Touring
4. don't share a room with Jimmy

5. definitely don't share a room with Jimmy and Trumpet!

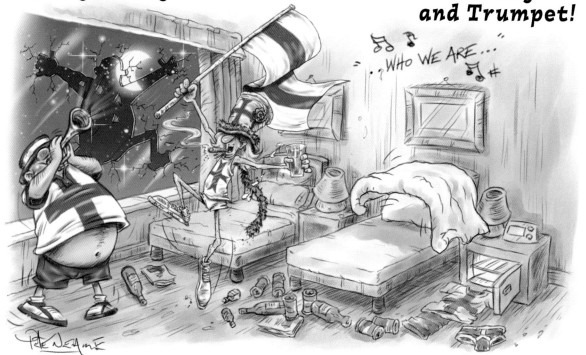

BARMY COMMENT: Singing

What is it about communal singing, Barmy style, that seems to bring out the party animal in all of us? In the midst of a bit of a 'sing along', I've seen even the deepest and most silent types suddenly take on the personality of Robbie Williams acting out 'Its A Mad Mad Mad Mad World' in a game of Charades.

Why is that? A case in point. Summer 2005. Traditionally - year in year out - I get together with a few of my ex-footballing/cricketing buddies to watch a couple of days at one of the Test matches. Blokes I don't see that often any more.

Anyway. We meet up. The conversation's a bit grim at first. Handshakes. Hellos. That sort of thing.

"Hello mate, you all right?"
"Not bad. How's things?"
"Not bad."
"Good."
"Yeah, good."
"Good...."

I know - shades of a Trappist Monk convention. And this is with people I've known for decades.

But - as sure as eggs come in shells - by lunchtime we'll be huddled together, heads thrown back, arms round shoulders, belting out a medley of our particular favourites like it's twenty years ago and we're back in some Cricket Clubhouse about to order up another Jug.

Now - fair play - a few Tinnies have probably gone down the neck by this point - but not enough to justify this Gremlin-type transformation. We even take requests. It's odd.

Now, another thing I've noticed, is that the level of approval, or that look of 'bxxxxxks, I'm sitting next to the mad loud bxxxxxds!!' tends to rise or fall relating to the type of songs that you sing.

Best idea. Stay away from anything that sounds like a football chant. For obvious reasons, a group of fattish ex- sporting types, singing pretty badly, tends to look and sound like a Cast Party for 'Lock, Stock and Two Smoking Barrels". People tend to get the wrong idea.

And now - while I'm on the subject of singing, and suitable material, there is something else I'd like to heave off my chest.

I think I've spoken elsewhere about the emotion everybody felt on the last day, Summer 2005, the Oval. Singing 'Jerusalem'. It was overwhelming.

Now, I'd like to ask one important question. Would the emotion and feeling have run quite so high if the number echoing around the Oval had been that well-known funereal dirge - 'God Save The Queen'? I seriously doubt it.

No - I swear - this is nothing to do with politics. That's not the point. The point is - it's dreary! For me, It stands

> **"Luckily cricket is one of the few sports where the players don't have to stand in a row before start of play and pretend to know the words or give a damn."**

alongside 'Mull of Kintyre" as one of the those songs that makes me want to crawl back into bed and pull the sheets over my head.

Luckily cricket is one of the few sports where the players don't have to stand in a row before start of play and pretend to know the words or give a damn.

But am I alone in the level of embarrassment before your average Rugby and Football international? England playing 'Outer Transylvania', or some such. Some country that probably has two pianos and an old mandolin between the whole population. And their National Anthem is some bouncy little number that you can see their players actually know the words to, and - good grief! - that they seem to enjoy. 'God Save the Queen' kicks off, and the boredom hangs over the stadium like a weather cloud over Lords. The England players either chew gum, and look off vacantly into the distance, or mouth the occasional word like so many goldfish trying to catch a breath. It's awful!

Imagine the difference if they were singing 'Jerusalem', or even 'Land of Hope and Glory' or, at a push, "Swing Low'!

If we put the awful music to one side for a moment - let's look at the words.

Now, for obvious reasons, this is one of those tunes that hides under the excuse of being 'anonymous'. No one wanted to take the blame, more like. Sometimes it's credited to a bloke called Henry Carey who is supposed to have written it around 1740 (I've just looked that up on Google - just in case you were impressed. 'Google' - what we now use instead of memory and a brain.) Anyway, poor old Henry is not around to deny the charge.

The lyrics. Come on! You can imagine old Henry lying there in his bath, when - splash! Eureka! - he gets the first line.

"God save our gracious Queen."

That's good, he thinks. Maybe I can write a National Anthem and I can retire from my job as Dung Collector or whatever. Maybe I'll wow the panel on the Elizabethan equivalent of Pop Idol.

Then - for the life of him - he can't think up the next bit. He puts the kettle on - has a coffee. Goes to the toilet. Kicks the cat. Then he thinks - I'll just repeat the first idea - just change it slightly.

"Long live our noble Queen."

He's happy now. Then, for the third line, in a burst of inspiration, he just repeats the first line again, only shorter.

"God save the Queen."

That's it - he's cracked it! He goes to the Tavern - gets pissed - sobers up - realises it's dreadful - calls it 'anonymous' - goes back to his dung job. So - what I'm getting at here - let's ditch it. Kick it out! Let's make 'Jerusalem' the National Anthem!!! All those in favour......?

YOUR MAN IN THE STANDS

Odd

Well, you asked for it, here's the Top Ten of mis-shapen cricketers – aye, that's the long & short of IT!

10 David Lawrence
(England, 5 Tests, 1988-1992)
Massive, David Lawrence was, massive. Absolutely huge. With a physique that looked as suited to turning people away from nightclub doors as it was to bowling fast, the Gloucestershireman was a popular and engaging figure on the county circuit throughout the eighties and into the nineties. And boy was he a big 'un.

9 Gus Logie
(West Indies, 52 Tests, 1983-1991)
Short-leg in the field, short of leg in general, Augustine 'Gus' Logie was arguably the greatest, in-front-of-the-bat close catcher of all time. An attacking right-handed batsman, un-surprisingly preferring to play on the back foot, Logie was an integral part of West Indies success throughout the eighties. Nothing looked funnier than seeing the Windies huddle up after taking a wicket with Logie looking as though he'd fallen out of giant Joel Garner's pocket.

8 Graham Gooch
(England, 118 Tests, 1975-1995)
If Graham Gooch had been born a woman, his ideal profession would undoubtedly have been barmaid, such was his top-heavy appearance. Renowned for his work ethic and fitness regime, 'Gray' has run many marathons and would drag himself around the ground at close of play on numerous laps of the square. Though sadly the ample chest sat uneasily on the figure, for England's highest ever run-getter was also the possessor of chicken's legs, as IT Botham never tired of pointing out.

7 Peter Such
(England, 11 Tests, 1993-1999)
Essex possessed in Peter Such and John Childs, one of county cricket's most potent spin attacks of the past 20 years. Childs, delivering his left-arm orthodox spin from a long straight run, and Such, flighting those off-breaks off a similarly long trot. But where Childs was all head down

and purposeful on his way to the wicket, Such was windmilling and, how can we put this, slightly effète in his manner. If England spin bowlers of the time were ever to be por-trayed as 'Carry On' charac-ters, Phil Tufnell would be played by Sid James, John Embury by Bernard Bresslaw and Peter Such would be Ken-neth Williams.

6 Lord Cowdrey of Tonbridge
(England, 114 Tests, 1954-1975)
Never has anyone made such an unathletic body shape look so at ease on a sports field. Cowdrey, born in Bangalore, India in 1934, the son of a tea planter and former first-class cricketer, was destined to play cricket given his initials of MCC. Rotund, exceptionally so in his later

Shaped Cricketers

years, flat feet, a moon face and a slightly worried look gave Cowdrey the manner of the perpetual schoolboy. Damn fine bat though.

5 Bruce Reid
(Australia, 27 Tests, 1985-1992)
Reid was the over-thin and gangly über-beanpole left-arm fast bowler who famously 'snapped in half' during the spoof commentary tape series, The Twelfth Man. A short but impressive career was seemingly blighted by injury at every turn. Reid is now a top-flight bowling coach, working very successfully last season at Hampshire. The Peter Crouch of fast bowlers, although there was no evidence to suggest Reid had a good touch for a big man.

4 Arjuna Ranatunga
(Sri Lanka, 93 Tests, 1982-2000)
Described as a stocky left-hander, but in truth Arjuna Ranatunga was a fat left-hander. Possessing as he did a haughty disposition at the crease and in the field, Ranatunga perfected the art of the walked single, arriving at the crease a split-second before the ball wherever it went in the outfield, in the process maximising the amount of walking paces he could take and infuriating the opposition. During a particularly hot one-day international at Sydney against Australia, Ranatunga called for a runner only to be knocked back by wicket keeper Ian Healy, who stated, not unreasonably, that "You don't get a runner for being an overweight, unfit, fat c***!"

3 Joel Garner
(West Indies, 58 Tests, 1977-1987)
Delivering the ball from above most sightscreens would be a tough enough challenge for most people. But add to that pace and steepling bounce, with the ball looking as if it could be used for ping-pong, and there you have a batting challenge few ever mastered. 'Big Bird', as he was affectionately known, was once asked admiringly by a female Australian fan if 'everything' about the giant Barbadian was in proportion. Garner replied to the contrary, saying that if that were the case he would stand 7'8" and not 6'8".

2 Trevor Franklin
(New Zealand, 21 Tests, 1983-1991)
Lanky, just plain lanky was Kiwi opener Trevor Franklin, and unlucky to boot, particularly when playing England. He broke a forearm in 1992, a thumb in 1986 and on his way home from that same ill-fated tour, managed to get himself mown down by a baggage trolley at Gatwick airport, shattering his over-long leg. Too lanky you see.

1 Ehteshamuddin
(Pakistan, 5 Tests, 1979-1982)
Madonna, Bono, Posh, Becks … Ehteshamuddin. When this former Test medium-pacer was plucked from Lancashire league obscurity to return to Test action against England at Headingley, it looked as if the call-up was somewhat unexpected. Even more so as the bus driver was opening the bowling alongside the great Imran Khan.
To describe the bowler as fat is to describe the invention of penicillin as handy. In fact, he was so lardy and unfit that he only managed 14 first innings overs before cramp set in, rendering him unable to bowl, field or contribute a single run in the remainder of his fifth and final Test. The mighty 'Sham' is currently on Pakistan's selection panel – we can't print a pic though, we do have young impressionable readers.....

TOP TEN

Horrorshow Injuries...

YOU KNEW IT WAS COMING. POUR YOURSELF A STIFF ONE AND MAKE YOURSELF COMFY, AS ALL OUT CRICKET'S PHIL WALKER BRINGS YOU CRICKET'S TEN CRUELLEST INJURIES.

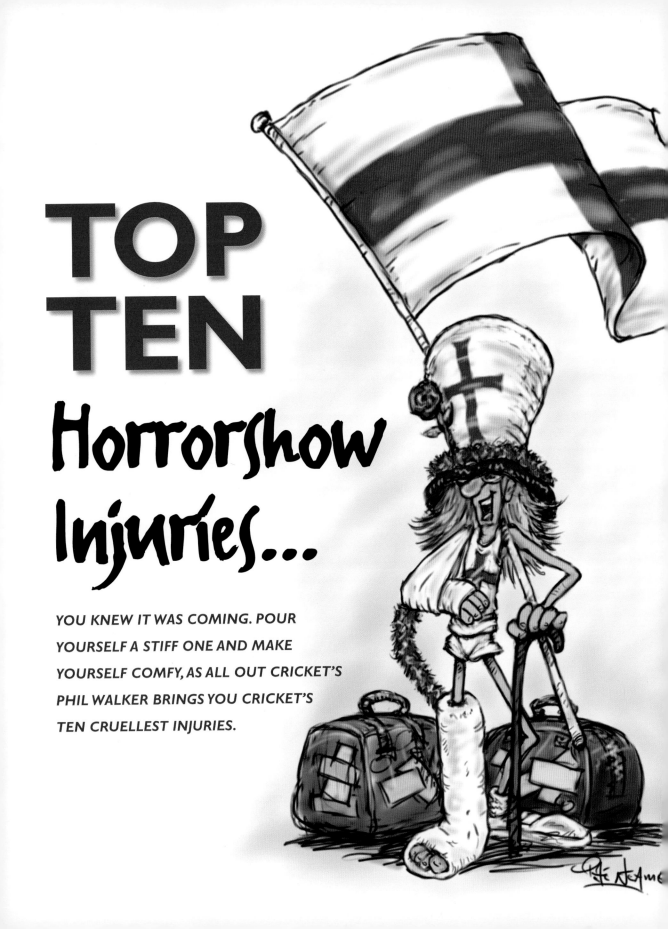

MIKE GATTING
(England, 79 Tests)

Growing up, other kids would say stuff like, "Oi, Walker! What d'ya like that crucket for? Fer poofs innit!" I'd smile wearily, gently shake my head, and draw to their attention deficit disorders a picture from my Wisden Cricket Annual 1986. I carried it around with me for this very purpose, you understand. I would then explain to these poor misguided youths as smugly as possible that if the game was so poncey, how come remnants of this gentleman's nose were still embedded in the ball after it made contact with his face? At 90mph. Chucked by a West Indian, 22 yards away.

PAUL DOWNTON
(England, 30 Tests)

In 1990 during a Sunday League game, Middlesex and England keeper Downton suffered a freak injury when a bail ricocheted into his eye. Although at first it looked innocuous, the impact damaged his vision to such an extent that he was forced to retire from the game the following season. One of county cricket's diamonds, it was a shockingly sad way to leave the game. At least he went on to earn a packet in the City.

RICKY PONTING
(Australia, 105 Tests)

First morning, Lord's, Ashes. No one can sit straight. It's just very edgy, everywhere. Questions swim around cluttered minds. One of them – will Stevie H do the business – needs an answer, because Punter's in, and the boy's a bit tasty against the short stuff. Harmison steams in down the hill and gives him a headshot. Ponting's barely halfway through the hook (he always takes it on) when it crashes into the side of his helmet. The impact on the grille is fierce enough to slash his cheek. Ponting doesn't flinch, just carries on. Harmison gets him soon after, but you still wouldn't know he was hurt. At close of play he heads off to see the plastic surgeon.

JUSTIN LANGER
(Australia, 100 Tests)

Cricket's harsh. Justin Clanger has spent a lifetime taking bruises for his country. Even on debut he's clunked by Ian Bishop, but Langer's a tough old boot and he staggers gamely through 99 Tests, rubbing this, nursing that, wearing one and hooking another, until finally, he scraps his way to Centurion Park, South Africa, and the big champers moment. Plaques, medals, good luck messages, the whole shebang. He writes in his

BBC column about the big day, how it's a unique, unforgettable moment in his life, how it means the world to him and his family… So what happens? He's hit flush on the skull first ball by Ntini, FIRST BALL, and rushed to hospital with concussion. He spends the remaining four days of his hundredth Test in a dark corner with a packet of peas on his barnet.

England player Q&A's

MATTHEW HOGGARD

Favourite film	Lord of the Rings
Favourite record	Kenny Rogers – Greatest Hits
Non-sporting hero	My wife Sarah
Football team	Not interested
Golf handicap	18
Favourite hair product	Banana Shampoo
Biggest fear	Burning alive
School subject	PE, Biology
First job	Kennel worker
Cricket idol	Allan Donald (SA)
First Ashes memory	Gatting's nose
Dream car	Kit from Knight Rider
Holiday destination	Malaysia
Favourite food	Steak/Chinese
Clothing brand	Anything that fits

"Growing up, other kids would say stuff like, 'Oi, Walker! What d'ya like that crucket for? Fer poofs innit!' I'd smile wearily, gently shake my head."

TERRY ALDERMAN
(Australia, 41 Tests)

"Never trust a have-a-go-hero," my mate always says, but then he's a coward. In the strange case of Terry Alderman, however, he may just have a point. Normally when a man feels compelled to remove his pants and flap around buck-naked across an outfield, all we get is Richie shaking his head, a fat steward in a lime green jacket, and a crowd loving the freakshow. But when England played Australia at Perth in 1981-82, Alderman saw fit to go after one such streaker with a rugby tackle. Top marks for gallantry, but surely when you're an international sportsman it's best to let the underclass sort out the mess. Or maybe this was his one chance to grab a naked man and he couldn't resist. Alderman damaged his right shoulder so badly that he didn't return to international cricket for over a year.

ANDY LLOYD
(England, 1 Test, 1984)

So, 33 minutes into his Test debut on his home ground (it could have been the medium pacers of New Zealand, or India's spinners), and England's Andy Lloyd ducks into a snaking bouncer from West Indies' Malcolm Marshall. Everyone falls silent. Marshall, a gentle man, winces. Lloyd is 10 not out. These are the only runs he will ever make for England. He doesn't pick up a bat again that season.

BERT OLDFIELD
(Australia, 54 Tests)

Cricket's most infamous haymaker. Bodyline time, and Harold Larwood digs one in to

Australian keeper Oldfield. It strikes his temple, the ball flies twenty yards to the off-side as the body staggers twice as far towards square-leg. He's carried from the field unconscious. Oldfield's response when he comes round? "My own fault." A touch of class. Bowler and batsman later become firm friends after Larwood emigrates, with delicious irony, to Australia.

DAVID 'SYD' LAWRENCE
(England, 5 Tests)

The saddest story of all on these pages. If he hadn't been so committed to representing his country, and so lovably, wildly enthusiastic about every ball he hurled down in her name, then Syd Lawrence would probably never have busted his left kneecap at the end of a flat, meandering Test match in New Zealand. Others would have looked at the dead-end game, throttled back, and maybe avoided such a grisly fate, but

Syd couldn't do that. It wasn't in his nature. It's why people loved him. Lawrence lands horribly in his delivery stride, a chilling shriek shooting out across the barren stands, and a promising career is in ruins.

SIMON JONES
(England, 18 Tests)

He's just got Langer for his first Ashes wicket, and Simon Jones, on his Ashes debut, is pretty pumped up. The ball passes him on its way to the boundary and Jones tears after it. He slides, technically perfect, just as he's been taught. His studs get caught in the soft, recently relaid turf, and the body buckles. The knee contorts, the body collapses, our hearts locate our mouths. It's bad, real bad. Doubts emerge for his career. As he's carried off a voice spits from the crowd: "Get up, you weak Pommie bastard." Two years later he sticks those words back where they came from. 21 Ashes wickets in four Tests.

STEVE WAUGH AND JASON GILLESPIE
(Australia, 168 Tests /Australia, 71 Tests)

Ready for this? Sri Lanka's Mahela Jayawardene top edges a sweep that goes miles up in the air. As it drops, Steve Waugh, running back, and Jason Gillespie, tearing in, both sprint to take the catch. Both sets of eyes are fixed on the skies. You know what's coming next, you can see it already… it's one of those moments in life when the awful truth prematurely unveils itself with nothing to halt its momentum… the two men collide, Dizzy's leg is obliterated on impact, and Waugh's nose gets splattered all over his face. Obviously Waugh says it's just a scratch. Horrifying. You don't want to see it. Honestly, you don't.

Cool Cricketers

Dust of your suede smoking jacket and spark up a gauloises, as All Out Cricket's Dan Benson gives you the top ten coolest cricketers! Nice...

10 W.G.Grace:
England, 22 Tests

Coolest trait: Beard

The beard. The gut. The ego. The arrogance (Umpire: "I'm afraid you're out, Dr Grace, sir." WG: "Am I sir? Am I? Am I buggery!!"). The doctorate which started when he was 19 and finished in his thirties with three kids, due to the amount of times he chose leather on wil-low over tonsillitis. The 839 runs in eight days, during a season in which only one other player passed the 1,000 run mark. The reappearance in 2005 as England's ghostly cheer-leader. The good Doctor.

9 Carl Hooper:
West Indies, 102 Tests

Coolest trait: The white sunhat

Cool Carl. So cool it's not even funny. Just watch the man bowl: two vaguely energetic steps, before thinking better of it and slowing the whole thing down. He strolls the last few yards. By the time he's in the 'delivery stride' – aka the 'seven-inch slide' – Carl looks thoroughly bored. The ball loops indifferently – far too slow, Carl – at the batsman's feet, and he's so unnerved by Carl's coolness that he's feeling sexually inadequate again and suddenly determined to whack the bugger out the ground. A leading edge, and Carl snaps a catch. He will then toss the ball four yards in the air behind him, or stick it in his pocket. When he bats he will hit three straight sixes off the quickest bowler in the match, and get caught at deep mid-wicket for a run-a-ball 78.

8 Derek Randall:
England, 47 Tests

Coolest trait: Madness

It was said of this man that he could catch swallows, which is quite an achievement. His speed and anticipation in the field made him the original Jonty Rhodes, except our 'Rags' could bat as well; his 174 at the MCG in 1977 was just stunning. When he took the catch to win the 1977 Ashes at Headingley, the boy did a cartwheel on the outfield. Plus, any man with the audacity to doff his cap to a bouncer from Dennis Lillee must possess the malaise of the mad and the neck of a giraffe, and that's enough to convince us that he's one cool cat. He'll probably wet himself when he sees his name in this list, but then how cool is that?

7 Shane Warne:
Australia, 135 Tests

Coolest trait: 659 Test wickets without running.

The talismanic face of Aussie cricket is renowned for playing with a smile and is adored by fans and players the world over. Indeed, add to this loveable façade a won-derfully chequered history ("...hair re-growth, anybody? Yeah? No wor-ries – I'll text you the number...") and you have a man who was only beaten by Fred in the popularity

← W.G. Grace:
"These people have not come to watch you bowl. They have come to watch me bat."

stakes this summer. He wears flares, and a pair of red boots nicked from a skittles alley. And he's the best bowler in the world, revolutionised the game. Which is cool. And he's a bit podgy, which is also cool. And his middle name is Keith, which is also…

6 Larry Gomes:
West Indies, 60 Tests
Coolest trait: Studio 54 perm and strip joint 'tache.
Wedged in at number three among the huge hitters and superstars of the last great West Indies team was the man with the wee mo' and the big 'fro. A slightly built but beautifully elegant stroke-maker, the opposition tended to underestimate Larry, but he was the little wise guy in the white suit surrounded by eight-foot heavies and mouthing off, giving it "you mess with me, punk, you mess with all of us". The Aussies took him on,

so he hit six hundreds. And his real name is Hilary, which is so ridiculous for a West Indian bloke cricketer that it has to be cool.

5 Douglas Jardine:
England, 22 Tests
Coolest trait: Superiority complex.
Douglas Jardine, Indian born of Scottish ancestry, was a splendidly pompous imperialist aristocrat. He was also the tactical genius who devised the Bodyline tactics in 1932-33 to neuter Bradman and his free-flowing pals. Jardine, England captain because he was posher than all but a hundred men alive (he was a terrible bat), directed humble pit-miner quick bowler Harold Larwood to remove the heads of those pesky convicts at the other end. Diplomatic relations took blows to the heart and head, questions were raised in parliament, Bradman halved his average, and England

won four out of five Tests. Jardine just puffed away on a Woodbine, and adjusted his neckerchief.

4 Keith Miller:
Australia, 55 Tests
Coolest line: "Pressure?" Pressure is having a Messerschmitt up your arse. Playing cricket is not." Fearless and erratic, Keith Miller remains the only man to have his name on both the bowling and batting honours board in the away dressing room at Lord's. Miller – World War II fighter pilot, high-society schmoozer, matinée idol, Corinthian – was a hugely successful all-rounder, who had the explosive ability to change games with a fiery spell or a merry whack. However, Michael Vaughan may not have completely agreed with his captaincy techniques, which were very much in keeping

with his character. While Vaughany constantly tinkers with his studied field settings, Miller opted for the more basic approach of huddling up his team then telling them to scatter! 'Nuff said.

3 Imran Khan:
Pakistan, 88 Tests
Coolest trait: Ask the ladies of Fulham. Pound-for-pound the coolest cricketer/man who ever lived. In the last ten years of Imran's career he played in 51 tests and averaged over 50 with the bat and under 19 with the ball. When you factor in his sickeningly handsome Adonis-features, the eligible bachelor in extremis status until his marriage to the beautiful Jemima Goldsmith, the title of most popular man in Pakistan, and a political career based on humanistic principles, you have all the ingredients for one of the most suave and complete players/men the game/world has ever seen.

2 Sir Vivian Richards:
West Indies, 121 Tests
Coolest trait: The swagger Viv Richards embodies cool. From that dramatic gum-chewing entrance, to the menacing stare down the ground at the bowler, right through to his ability to hook the ball off the end of his nose with nothing but pride and a maroon cap to protect him, Viv is cool. Even now he possesses the refined dignity to look and sound sophisticated, down-to-earth and laid back, all at then same time. He was once forced into a chat with an AOC writer, and his first words were: "Hello, I'm Vivian." Now that's cool.

1 Richie Benaud:
Australia, 60 Tests
Coolest trait: Cream suits Morning everyone… As a leg-spinning all-rounder Richie Benaud, with his 246 wickets, was simply brilliant. As peerless captain in 28 Tests, he never lost a series. As a commentator, he is untouchable. He is the game's most cherished voice. Shane Warne cites him as his biggest influence. An Aussie team-mate once remarked that if Rich fell in a lorry-load of shit, he'd still come up smelling of roses. His last words as a commentator in England: "…and now in the commentary box, Mark Nicholas and Tony Greig…" – modest, spare, ironic, Arlottesque, cool. Is he real? Who knows. Richie Benaud, the coolest man in the world.

GOING ON TOUR:
The Essential Barmy Army Guide To Touring
6. check out the wild life

BARMY COMMENT:
Sports Nuts

Being part of the Barmy Army means being surrounded by Sports Nuts for hours at a time. Our Man In The Stands takes a red-eyed look at the phenomenon...

True story. My eldest boy was five years old. So I thought - it's about time he put aside childish things and got into grown up adult pursuits. So, first off, I lifted him out of his pram - took him to the Pub .

Next up - Cricket! I thought, yeah, he's probably about ready to share the joys of sitting on the sofa for days at a stretch and watching England batting (okay - 'hours' at a stretch!).

So, one momentous day, I had a few like-minded souls around, so I sat my boy in between Russ and Andy T, whilst not of course letting Ged breathe anywhere near him (that's for alcohol reasons - not halitosis!)

Now, apart from having no money to join in the Sweep (we accepted his Game Boy as collateral) he fitted in

like a hand in a pair of batting gloves. Good lad!

Now England were bowling at the time and, if my memory serves me correctly, one of those dour jutting-chin South Africans was at the crease. Could have been Jacques Kallis. A man who puts the 'apart' in 'apartheid'.

Anyway - hats thrown in the air - we got him! Cue my boy's Daddy - me - leaping to my feet - pumping the air with my fist - yelling 'yes yes yes!!!' - and generally acting like a cross between someone with Tourettes Syndrome and one of those Morris Dancer blokes you get in pub gardens on Bank Holidays.

Now. obviously, my boy was used to me, his Dad. He'd known me, after all, every since he

was a baby. He'd seen me giving the glad eye to one of his cute teachers - yes. Being read the riot act by my wife for once getting on a train and leaving my son on the platform - yes. But he had never seen me in Sport Spectator mode.

He began to wail like Shane Warne being hit by a strawberry.

To suddenly realise that his father, the Rock and Comfort of his life, was just as odd and capable of acting wierdly as that girl he sat next to in class who insisted on peeing on the floor instead of the toilet. Imagine the shock!

Which brings me, dragging my feet, to my point. Which is? Well, it made me realise how odd some of our behaviour must seem to those people

← Sales of Aftersun went through the roof

for whom sporting events aren't the fulcrum of the year. In plain English, to those unfortunates (or maybe fortunates) who don't give a toss about sport we sports nuts must seem nuts.

What is it about seeing Jacques Kallis being bowled that makes me act like Screaming Lord Sutch on a day when he's forgotten to take his medication?

Let me consider. Now I could go all pompous and talk about sport providing perfect moments, but I won't.

I think it's more to do with the notion of being English - the fact that we have been put through the grinder so many times that we have learnt - why not - to enjoy our brief successes when they come along.

We all know that feeling you get watching an England batting collapse. Like getting on to the last train home after an evening composed of about eight or nine pints - desperate for a lash - and then realising that actually the train that you've boarded doesn't have a toilet. It's a mixture of panic, pain and horror made all the greater by an acute awareness of the greater panic, pain and horror still to come. (Anyone who ever got on

the Shepperton train from Waterloo knows what I'm talking about.)

And anyone who sat through the recent England - Northern Ireland defeat will understand why, after watching England beat Germany 5-1, in Germany, why I spend the next two or so hours calling up everyone I knew and yelling '5-1!' down the phone. I even called my Godmother, and the last time we met she'd been holding me over a Font while some bloke in black poured water all over my head. And Summer, 2005. Bejesus!!!

The Oval. The last day. We'd just won. The whole ground was singing Jerusalem, except me. I couldn't get the words out. I was so choked up. Now I'm a fairly emotional bloke in the normal course of events anyway - I tend to well up if the milkman delivers the correct number of pints - so this was all too much for me.

Now at some point in the near future I'm going to have to have a long heart to heart with my boy about the joys, and sadnesses (there seems a lot of 'S's in that word?) of watching our England teams. Already I've noticed how he copies his Dad and leaps around the room, yelling and pumping his fist. He does it at all the wrong

moments of course, but what the hell?

In the words of the Bulldog out of Tom and Jerry - Spike (yes it's not all cricket with me - I do know other cultural references) - in Spike's immortal words - "Dat's my boy!"

Although, in truth, part of me is sorry that he will have to go through it all - all that agony - just for one or two summers like the last one. Ah well... And, just as an afterthought, doesn't Jacques Kallis look a bit like Spike the Bulldog. Something about that chin? Whatever....

YOUR MAN IN THE STANDS

Balmy Army

Everywhere we go... wish you were here

Watch England play abroad with their most passionate supporters.
Wherever they go, we won't be far behind.

All tour packages are offered on our website

www.barmyarmy.com Or call 0845 061 0612 for further details

Competitively priced and good value for money, we offer trips for groups of all sizes as well as solo
travelers. Barmy Army Travel is fully ABTA, ATOL and IATA bonded.

BALLS OF STEEL

As a reaction to Brett Lee's ability to produce three of the game's most lethal deliveries at will or accidentally, AOC looks at the most evocative deliveries in cricket – wicket-taking, legal or otherwise. Much deliberation, thought, cajoling and provocation produced the list of the ten most devastating delivery types in the game…

⑩ THE NIPBACKER-KNACKER-CRACKER
(aka taking one in the bread basket, family jewels or plums)

**Wicket-taking potential: ★★
(can on occasions unluckily
drop from body onto stumps)
Batsman discomfort: ★★★★
Long term effects: ★★
Rarity: ★
Shock value: ★**

SUMMARY: Many a young player's career has begun, and effectively ended, the first time they cop one 'downstairs'. As painful as it sounds, the nipbacker-knacker-cracker is the delivery that causes more mirth on the field than anything in the game. As the ball strikes the body there are always two sounds – a muffled 'pfumph' followed by a low-pitched groan. Or a hearty clonk, followed by the same guttural emission. The first scenario registers a near miss, the second a bull's eye; with the ball making 'full-on' contact with the most primitive of protective wear, the box*.

When this happens, the game stops. Everyone, umpires and non-stricken batsmen included, snigger as the 'winded' player initially crouches down to relieve the rising symptoms of nausea, before ending up prone on all fours then proceeding to bite chunks of turf out off the return crease as the testicular toothache intensifies.

Play is generally suspended as a 'magic' drink of water is called for. "Don't rub 'em, count 'em" is always proffered by some wag or other and the prospect of copping a second one in the nuts doesn't bear thinking about.

There are rarely many long-term effects, other than the batsman having to sporadically transport his now even more horribly distended and swollen 'meat and two veg' in a wheelbarrow.

*or manhole cover, as it is known amongst women cricketers.

⑨ THE LEG-SIDE WIDE
(aka rubbish)

**Wicket-taking potential: 0
Batsman discomfort: ★★★
Long term effects: ★★★
Rarity: 0
Shock value: 0**

SUMMARY: At the apex of the sport, the leg-side wide is an easy rule to apply and done so superbly by top-flight umpires. The ball is bowled behind the batsman's legs, and however close to the pad, it's a wide. Everyone knows the score. Everyone knows it's not a good delivery. It's a wide. Simple.

But at club level, it can be an absolute nightmare. The first inkling of impending trouble comes in the first over of the game. The still stiff opening bowler runs up, delivers the first ball that bobbles down the leg-side where it's fielded on the third bounce by the scrabbling wicket-keeper. The umpire charitably smiles at the player, allowing him to get

away with the loosener. From there on it becomes a free-for-all.

Endless deliveries leak down the leg-side untouched by the flailing batsman. The umpire has now set out his parameters of tolerance and in doing so he lets the big quick complete his opening spell of six dreadful overs for a mere 11 runs.

The phrase 'same for both sides' is never part of the equation, especially when the first ball of the second innings also sails away down the leg side, this time called by an umpire who has by now been participating in the game for three hours and is feeling a bit more part of the action. All hell breaks loose. From here, every ball is faced with the levels of scrutiny normally only the preserve of a high court judge.

It's the inconsistency of application that makes this 'nothing going for it' delivery a potential incendiary device. And why it makes our top ten of lethal deliveries.

 THE GOOGLY
(aka the 'Bosie' or the 'wrong 'un')
Wicket-taking potential: ★★★
Batsman discomfort: ★★★
Long term effects: ★★
Rarity: ★★★
Shock value: ★★

SUMMARY: Being bowled out when padding up to a googly has to be the most humiliating dismissal in cricket. Stood at the crease with the bat held aloft watching incredulously as a leg break turns into an off break, thud-

ding straight into pad or stump. And it all seems to happen in slow motion.

I don't care who you are, very few people can genuinely pick a leg break from a googly – it's too complicated a mathematical equation to be done in less than half a second.

From the point where any dumb-founded batsman walks off to the end of the innings, every incoming batsman is wary and fails to put away endless long hops as they

Taking one on the thumb end... Everyone knows how much that hurts – so much so that batsmen are reluctant to take their glove off to check the damage.

watchfully steer the ball into the off side for fear of it turning the opposite way.

Even terrible leg spinners, if they bowl a googly, strike fear into the hearts of batsmen. Because, even if you feel you're on top, it just may end in absolute humiliation…

 THE LIFTER
(aka the spitting cobra)
Wicket-taking potential: ★★★★
Batsman discomfort: ★★★★
Long term effects: ★★★★
Rarity: ★
Shock value: ★

SUMMARY: During an excessively wet or dry spell of weather, pushing forward and taking the odd ball on the gloves pretty well goes with the territory. But on good wickets, the 'it came from nowhere' lifter is a veritable firework through the letterbox. Taking one on the thumb end from

a fast bowler is another rite of passage for a player. Everyone knows how much that hurts – so much so that batsmen are reluctant to take their glove off to check the damage. From the administration of cold spray onwards, the next few deliveries are all potential wicket-takers as the batsman now hangs back in his crease, afraid of reaching too far forward. A batsman coping with the lifter/grubber combination (see no.3 on the list) has to be one of the finest sights in the game.

 THE YORKER
(aka the sandshoe crusher or homing pigeon)
Wicket-taking potential:
★★★★★
Batsman discomfort: ★★★
Long term effects: ★
Rarity: ★★
Shock value: ★

SUMMARY: When bowled with real pace, the yorker looks an unplayable ball, especially when allied to the excessive reverse swing of a Wasim Akram or Waqar Younis. At best the batsman may hope to jab down on the ball and squirt it through their legs or down to third man for runs. At its most lethal, the ball cannons from the boot ends and into the stumps. As the batsman returns to the pavilion and removes his foot-wear, he finds claret seeping through his socks where the delivery has scorched through the mesh of his modified trainers, leaving the player to think 'where were the steel toecaps when they were needed?'

When a quickie can bowl them to order, the batsman is in for a rough time, especially at the tail end of an innings. Bats are broken, toes are broken and hearts are broken, as never enough wood is making contact with the ball to keep any run chase alive.

5 THE BOUNCER

(aka the bumper, bomb-er or 'bit of pepper')
Wicket-taking poten-tial: ★★★★
Batsman discomfort: ★★★★
Long term effects: ★★
Rarity: ★★★
Shock value: ★★

SUMMARY: Bouncers are not the preserve of club cricket. It happens about once a season and anyone who fancies themselves as having 'a few

wheels on their wagon' is likely to get reported for intimidatory bowling by doddery umpires and whingeing batsmen.

When a club cricketer is stood in a pub with pint in hand and he says, 'I love it, me – it gets me going' referring to facing the short sharp stuff, don't believe a word of it. They've obviously never been faced with a real going over.

Many players have faced long hops, some have faced the odd short ball on a bouncy wicket, but few have found themselves in the firing line for the real roughhouse treatment of a bumper barrage.

It is harrowing to be on the receiving end, but fascinating to watch. There is nothing more manly than taking on a quick bowler, and nothing more cowardly than complaining about it. Cricket is played with a hard ball and fear becomes part of that equation. If you don't like the heat…

4 THE BEAMER

(aka the head hunter)
Wicket-taking potential: 0
Batsman discomfort: ★★★★★
Long term effects: ★★★★★
Rarity: ★★★★
Shock value: ★★★★★

SUMMARY: Not an easy ball to bowl deliberately; neither physically nor emotionally. To make the decision to beam someone can never be taken lightly and certainly not made with any clarity of thought. It occasionally happens in the heat of the moment, when a bowler feels completely powerless or wrongly done to and sees his only means of redressing any control of a situation lies in let-ting the batsman have a 'flat 'un'.

When on target, the batsman is more often than not unsighted as he instinctively looks down the pitch at the point of release for the spot on the pitch where his brain computes the ball will land. When the ball isn't there – it's often down to luck whether the batsman avoids the ball or not.

Beamers make emotions that are already running high, run even higher. There is no place for them in any form of the sport. Oddly the term of deliberately pitching the ball at a batsman in baseball is known as hav-ing been 'beaned'.

3 THE GRUBBER

(aka the pea roller, shooter, startled mouse or guzzunder)
Wicket-taking potential: ★★✍ ★★★
Batsman discomfort: ★★★
Long term effects: ★★
Rarity: ★★★
Shock value: ★★

SUMMARY: Arguably, there is a no more nailed on wicket-taker in the game than a good old-fashioned worm burner. The sound of the ball hitting the very base of a set of stumps is a thing of wonder. A solid, all absorbing 'bonk' on contact, with the ball either remaining rested in amongst the disturbed furniture or

Taken from All Out Cricket magazine, available from WHSmith or subscribe at www.alloutcricket.co.uk

gently rolling back into the area where batsmen take their guard. Lovely.

So unplayable is the ball, especially when bowled at pace, that few survive it. You can have been at the crease for as long as you like, but when that short of a length ball shoots along the ground and across the top of the boot straps, it has a poetic feel all of its own.

Any cricketer worth their salt has suffered; lamented and finally gone on to sing the 'Pea Roller Blues'. Amen to that, brother.

West Indies cricket was said to be brought up on young men throwing the ball at each other to generate added pace during games of beach cricket.

② THE THROW

(aka the pelt or chuck)
Wicket-taking potential: ★★★★
Batsman discomfort: ★★★★
Long term effects: ★★★★★
Rarity: ★★★★
Shock value: ★★★★★

SUMMARY: Much has been written lately about chuckers in the game – whether they are or not. But elsewhere in cricket, bowlers go unreported, but never without scrutiny from their playing peers.

The bowler that throws gains an advantage over conventional actions. Not only do they benefit from added spin or pace, but they also profit from the inability of batsmen to line up the likely trajectory when the bowler releases the ball.

Bowled with a straight arm, it is reasonably straightforward to predict where the arm is likely to

THE MANKAD

(aka the run out backing up)
Wicket-taking potential: 0
Batsman discomfort: ★ ★ ★ ★ ★
Long term effects: ★ ★ ★ ★ ★
Rarity: ★ ★ ★ ★ ★
Shock value: ★ ★ ★ ★

SUMMARY: Being run out backing up is now banned in cricket, but has remained a recognised mode of dismissal in the indoor game; where it goes in the scorebook as a 'Mankad'.

The term derives from the name of Indian Test player Vinoo Mankad. On his country's 1947/48 tour of Australia he ran out Bill Brown backing up in the second Test; after having done the same thing to Brown in an earlier game. Infuriated, the Australian media coined the phrase that someone dismissed in this way was said to have been 'Mankaded'. The practice, since outlawed, in no small part due to the amount of fights that invariably break out when someone runs through the crease and whips a bail off behind a batsman's back in club cricket.

Although a non-delivery by definition, the failure to release the ball is seen as the most cowardly of acts by all but the hardest nosed of players. In cricket circles, I suspect that the act of mankading someone is reviled ahead of sleeping with a team-mate's wife, repeatedly pinching the bowling when batting; or even worse – not taking your turn on the roller when preparing Saturday's pitch. When it occurs an atmosphere not unlike that of a 30-man bench-clearing brawl, the preserve of ice hockey, ensues. Although generally pulling up just short of a fully fledged fist fight, re-lations between the clubs involved never fully recover.

The Mankad... evocative term with the most underhand connotations – something I'm sure 'Our Vinoo' may regret.

appear in view when the bowler circles his arm. But for the bowler that throws, this isn't the case. The ball is released from an odd angle, making it appear in the batsman's viewfinder from somewhere unexpected.

West Indies cricket was said to be brought up on young men throwing the ball at each other to generate added pace during games of beach cricket. The reality was that it only took one of these recreational cricketers to be able to get their arm straight and there was a world-class paceman in the making. When playing these fun games amongst the waves, everyone throws – on the greens and parks of England, throwing is a whole different kettle of jerk pork, curried goat and flying fish.

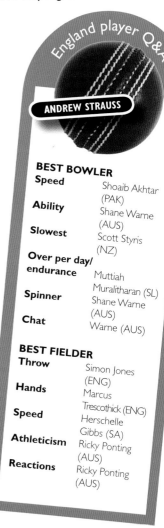

England player Q&A's

ANDREW STRAUSS

BEST BOWLER

Speed	Shoaib Akhtar (PAK)
Ability	Shane Warne (AUS)
Slowest	Scott Styris (NZ)
Over per day/ endurance	Muttiah Muralitharan (SL)
Spinner	Shane Warne (AUS)
Chat	Warne (AUS)

BEST FIELDER

Throw	Simon Jones (ENG)
Hands	Marcus Trescothick (ENG)
Speed	Herschelle Gibbs (SA)
Athleticism	Ricky Ponting (AUS)
Reactions	Ricky Ponting (AUS)

BARMY COMMENT: Sledging

One of the interesting talking points of Summer 2005 was the new Australia stance on sledging. In other words, Ponting and his boys trying to take on the personality of Sister Maria Theresa. Now much as I applaud this 'about face', I think that the Aussies - poor things - have been surprised at the fact that we do not suddenly accept them in this new and flattering light.

I don't know about you but the notion of the Aussies promoting fair play is tantamount to the Romans, after years of throwing the Christians to the Lions, suddenly displaying an interest in flower arranging. Or the Elephant Man promoting a skin care product. Or Hannibal Lecter lecturing on vegetarianism. Oliver Reed promoting the joys of orange juice. You get the idea. Basically - it won't wash!

There's also the fact that to the Aussies sledging traditionally means the verbal equivalent of being kicked in the head, and about as subtle. A typical exchange between two Aussies might go something like this:

"Hey, mate, you're a fat fxxxxxx bxxxxxx!"

"Who are you calling a fat fxxxxxx bxxxxxx?!"

"You! You're a fat fxxxxxx bxxxxxx!"

"No, you are!"

"No, mate, you are!"

"You are!"

This might go on until both of them collapse with brain fatigue, or one of the least Australian of the onlookers calms them down with some raw meat, or giving them some beads and coloured glass to play with.

You think I am exaggerating. Let me quote from a recorded exchange between Merv Hughes, one of the more notorious sledgers of our time, and the great West Indian, Viv Richards. Now, fair play to Merv, our Viv is not actually the first person I would choose to take on in a verbal exchange. This is a man who has muscles in his hair. But after a few deliveries where Viv might have played and missed a bit, Merv decided to stare the great man down. After a while, Viv had had enough.

"This is my island, man, my culture. Don't you be staring at me. In my culture we just bowl."

Merv said nothing until he actually bowled Viv out. Then as Viv walked away he said:

"Well, mate, in my culture, we just say fxxx off!"

Now, again, 'fair play'! Not bad. But it would, of course, be funnier if it wasn't quite so close to the truth.

There's also the habit - the verbal tic - that it seems is common to all Aussies. That's the trick, already noted here, of saying 'mate' in every sentence, As if that makes it all okay. As if that excuses everything, whatever:

"Oh mate, I've just run over your wife and kids, and burnt your house down, Oh mate...."

And finally, if we're picking on the poor Aussies, let's reserve space for another great man taking the moral high ground - Shane Warne. Do we all remember the fuss Shane made about being hit by a strawberry whilst fielding on the boundary? Now, don't get me wrong, I'm dead against anything being thrown on to the pitch at any time, but a strawberry? Maybe, if it was a genetically modified strawberry the size of a melon, then yes, I'd complain.

"Oh mate, I've just run over your wife and kids, and burnt your house down, Oh mate...."

Or if it was still in the tin, maybe. But a strawberry? Come on Shane, get a sense of perspective!

Let's put Shane's reaction against the treatment meted out to Freddie Flintoff in the same situation when in Aus. Correct me if I'm incorrect, but I think something more than strawberries were chucked on to the pitch on that occasion, and I don't remember Freddie bleating about it.

Anyway, as I've said, if Ponting and the boys are trying to change the kind of National stereotypes I've portrayed in this article, then good on them. But equally they can't expect the last fifteen or so years just to be swept under the rain covers and forgotten.

Also, in the end, do we really want to be playing against 'nice' Australians? The idea that Australians are poor sports and horrible to play against is as deep rooted in our culture as the idea that Germans nick the sun loungers, and American women of a certain age have large bottoms. And, in a sense, where's the pantomime without the pantomime villain? And didn't we enjoy our victory - summer 2005 - all the more because Glen McGrath played the bad man and predicted a five nil thrashing.

Fair play, Glen mate, but it wasn't only your ankle that was twisted......

YOUR MAN IN THE STANDS

TOP TEN

We weighed up the pros and cons and came up with this list of gadgets, gizmos and goodies that have all had a profound influence on the cricketing landscape.

REVERSE SWING

Okay, so not strictly technological as we may know it, but it is cricket technology and a bit scientific, so it works for us. And we can bowl it, bat against it and nearly explain it. And the Aussies… err, can't.

MODERN BATTING PADS

Lightweight with Velcro fastenings, and allows you to get hit on the legs without breaking them, as opposed to the good old canvas and cane version. The old style leg-guards were exactly the same as the modern pad apart from the fact that they were too heavy, offered no protection and when hit on the buckles that held them in place by the ball it sent an 'electric shock' through your kneecap and down into your boots.

AEROPLANES

Can you imagine how Australia's David Boon would have felt, arriving in the UK after six weeks on the Good Ship Lollipop? If he drank 52 cans during the 30-hour Sydney to London flight, a six-week boat trip would have seen him down 1747 tinnies. So pretty rough then.

TECHNOLOGICAL ADVANCES...

SKY TV

The opportunity to watch cricket all over the world all through the night. What did we do before it?

THE NATIONAL CRICKET CENTRE, LOUGHBOROUGH

£4.5 million is nothing in the context of providing a much needed one-stop-shop of everything you need to play cricket for England.

DROP-IN PITCHES

Soil meticulously watered and grass seed lovingly nurtured to within an irrelevance of perfection – all done in a 'laboratory' environment away from possible wear, tear and natural disaster. Simply winched into place when ready to use. Now that's clever.

MERLYN

The bowling machine used by the England team to recreate Shane Warne's varied spins and trajectories during the Ashes campaign. Worked a treat, as the batsmen restricted the world's most famous rug wearer to 40 wickets at 19 apiece!

"If he drank 52 cans during the 30-hour Sydney to London flight, a six-week boat trip would have seen him down 1747 tinnies."

THE THIRD UMPIRE.

Takes the heat off the standing umpire by reviewing run outs that are nigh on impossible to assess with the naked eye without compromising his position of authority. Brilliant.

HOVER COVERS

Takes seconds to cover the pitch with little effort. Fancy one for your local village ground? Expect to pay about 100 grand.

FLOODLIGHTS

Turns cricket from a great game into a great spectacle.

...AND THE CLUNKERS

THE ANAL CYST
(sorry, Analyst)

Highlighting just how Flintoff has bowled his last two deliveries from three centimetres wider on the crease... How one right-arm bowling action looks like another... And how all Test batsmen could avoid getting out, should they have had prior knowledge on what the ball was going to do. All of this introduced from just down the road from a bloke in a truck, courtesy of Simon Hughezzzz.

REFERRING CATCHES TO THE THIRD UMP

Third Umpire – good thing. Referring catches to him, when TV replays, looked at from a dozen different angles and slowed down to a thousand frames per second, are still inconclusive – bad thing. Let the men in the middle sort that one out. And by men in the middle, we include the players in that too.

STUMP CAM

Great if you want to look at the straps on the back of Andrew Strauss' pads. Useful for showing the weather at the time of a batsman's dismissal – off-stump knocked flat on its back to reveal the sky.

"Lost forever, the metallic 'ching, ching, ching' sound that accompanied a boundary from the good old manual score box."

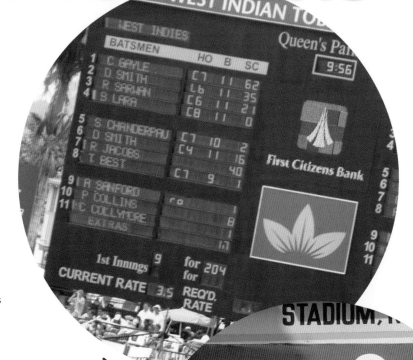

→ Dodgy electronic Scoreboards... what's wrong with the good old fashioned manual ones?!

ELECTRONIC SCOREBOARDS

Lost forever, the metallic 'ching, ching, ching' sound that accompanied a boundary from the good old manual score box. And the electric one packs up every other session, whereupon the dinky manual one gets wheeled out. And guess what? The little fella always works!

ALUMINIUM BATS

Never mind Dennis, nice try…

MUSICAL STABS

Seven seconds of random muzak after a boundary – "You messed about, I caught you out, Howzat?" – wrong from every conceivable angle.

COMMENTATOR CAM

What's all that about?

MEANINGLESS STATISTICS

Producers seem to enjoy filling the screen full of meaningless stats, leaving a third of the television for the action. Is anyone interested in cricket in 1881/82, when England scored 124-6 in the second innings to win the game… With information available like that I'm sure Ladbrokes are quaking in their boots.

> "You messed about, I caught you out, Howzat?"

England player Q&A's

MATTHEW HOGGARD

BEST FIELDER

Throw	Simon Jones
Hands	Andrew Flintoff
Speed	Herschelle Gibbs (SA)
Athleticism	Paul Collingwood
Reactions	Mohammed Kaif (IND)
Bravery	Anyone at silly point/short leg

THE DUAL-FACED BAT

Some dull spark came up with the idea of a bat that had a flat face on both sides making it much easier to alter the shot to a reverse sweep at the last moment. Not so useful however if you want a bat with a middle in it, available in the playing of every other shot.

LIGHT METERS

Does anybody actually know why we use these bloody things? Either it's dark or it's not!

"In the Barmy world of mobile, we'll find the right deal 4u..."

James Anderson
THE KNACK

Photo: All Out Cricket

After a tough tour of South Africa in 2004-05, James Anderson dropped back into the ranks of county cricket to rediscover the form that made him at one time English cricket's hottest property. Andy Afford went to the National Cricket Centre at Loughborough to see if the Lancastrian was ready to re-establish himself as an international player.

"I reckon he'll drive something that's a little bit flash – a two-seater. Something fast, certainly."

"No way. He's well northern. A Burnley lad. Lancashire through and through. It'll be dead steady. Definitely four doors. He'll drive a club car. A Vauxhall Vectra. Nothing more certain."

The above speculation about James Anderson's likely mode of transport is an interesting one. And an indication as to the contradictions he throws up. On the one hand, he is your archetypal local boy made good – he's from a cricketing background in the heartland of his native county. But on the other there's his appearance. Particularly when sporting, as he did, the forerunner of the Kevin Pietersen™ Uber-skunk hairdo, that at its most incendiary was a homemade scarlet derivation. That haircut alone screamed that he'd be behind the wheel of something a bit racy.

I'm waiting for him at the re-named National Cricket Centre at Loughborough, where he and the rest of his England teammates have been fine tuning, training and blowing away the cobwebs in advance of a winter to be spent on the subcontinent. The England man drifts languidly out of a team meeting that has overrun by 40

minutes and he happily informs me that he now knows all the whys and wherefores of the current thinking on match-fixing and drug-taking in the sport.

There isn't a cricketer, dead or alive, who hasn't some form of superstition or quirk. And as we begin walking and talking, he looks back at the latter stages of the first chapter of his international career with a nice touch of irony: "I did wonder whether it was the red hair's fault…(smiles the broadest of smiles)"

He doesn't mean it…obviously. But cricketers are a funny lot. And looking back at the Ashes last season, let alone Anderson's stop-start career, there may be something in it. After all, it took the reconfiguring of Kevin Pietersen's barnet from the 'run-less' blue version, back to his 'natural' peroxide before the urn was secured. Maybe there's more to it than you may think.

Anderson is currently 'barnet intacto'; free of the highlights, shaven head, DIY colourings, additives, e-numbers or preservatives of his hair's well-documented past. His clothes are the uniform of the young and affluent cricketer – jeans, t-shirt and work boots. The ensemble doesn't look expensive, but you know it is. He wears a ring on the third finger of his left hand, only an engagement ring I'm told, and something (with now the broadest grin imaginable) he has been

"I reckon Simon Jones' top half. And Andre Nel's legs would be good, they're like tree trunks. Fred's pace – ball upon ball, spell after spell. Glenn McGrath's accuracy and Steve Harmison's slower ball... but don't tell him that!"

informed by his fiancée that everyone is wearing nowadays. And as for the car? An Audi A4 convertible. Well swift… but not ever so flashy.

Physically the Lancastrian is deceptive. Incredibly lean for a modern-day cricketer, he's short of beanpole height at 6'2", but all arms and legs. He has the torso that would uncharitably be referred to as a diver's dream – possessing as he does a sunken chest. And as we walk down to the net area I ask jokingly if Anderson had considered asking Santa for a set of pecs and shoulders for Christmas: "I think it would help (laughs)." He agrees, adding further: "I try to put weight on – I eat all sorts of rubbish, but never seem to really stack it on. It is something that Troy (Cooley, England's bowling coach) and the management team keep saying. It would be great to have Simon Jones' upper body."

While we're on the subject of attributes, I ask Anderson what elements of other bowlers he thinks might make the perfect composite quickie. He runs with the theme: "Physically, as I said, I reckon Simon Jones' top half. And Andre Nel's legs would be good, they're like tree trunks. Fred's pace – ball upon ball, spell after spell. Glenn McGrath's accuracy and Steve Harmison's slower ball... but don't tell him that!"

It is well-documented that Anderson

had a tough time last winter in South Africa with England. After no cricket to speak of, he was drafted into the crucial fourth Test side at Johannesburg and figures of 2-117 and 0-32, although disappointing, do not tell the full horror. He bowled all over the place. Herschelle Gibbs, caught at third man off a delivery that could have been called a wide, and Mark Boucher succumbing in similar vein but at cover, were his two strangles. England, courtesy of a second innings 7-61 from Matthew Hoggard, won the match and went ahead in the series, but it was little consolation for the young speedster. Anderson, as an international cricketer, had hit rock bottom.

There followed very public discussion about him being thrown back into Test cricket after little match time of any sort in the previous 18 months, although he'd done a power of net bowling. The consensus of opinion that a full season of county cricket (up until last season Anderson had only bowled 800 first-class overs in total) would aid the rehab. Anderson speaks fondly of his return to domestic action: "Playing at Lancashire, after the tour I had, was great. I loved it being back there away from the cameras. I got back to bowling, which is something I love to do. I even love bowling in the nets – but not for the sake of it as had happened in the past. What do I love about bowling? I love bowling well

and bowling a great ball and making the batsman look stupid when you get them out. I suppose, I do actually really like the showing off side of playing." We both laugh at this revelation – there's that contradiction again.

As a bowler, James Anderson has a 'win big – lose big' style. Anyone who pitches the ball up to the bat, as he does, runs the risk of being driven to the boundary. And as quick as any

bowler might be, there isn't a batsman in the world who doesn't fancy a dart at a ball when it's pitched up.

And when the young Anderson pitched the ball up, as he did during his early international appearances, at 90mph and swinging the ball away from the right-hander, he proved nigh on unplayable. For the batsman, what was a good delivery and what bad were blurred to the point of being unfathomable. What appeared to be a four-ball, four-fifths of the way down the pitch, ended up knocking the off pole flat on its back as players worked to leg.

And it was this style of 'miracle ball' bowling that made James Anderson such hot property in 2003. He was drafted into England's one-day side after a fantastic spell with the England Academy squad, then accommodated in Adelaide. He'd bowled beautifully out there and Duncan Fletcher wanted him as a replacement for a myriad of pace bowling injuries. He came in and did brilliantly almost immediately.

In recent times, I can't remember a more perfect spell of swing bowling than the one produced at Newlands in Cape Town against Pakistan during 2003's World Cup in Southern Africa. After England had posted a competitive, but not impregnable 248-8 in their 50 overs, Anderson produced an opening spell of 4-28 from 10 unchanged overs. It was mesmeric. After watching Shoaib Akhtar bowl the first 'TV recognised' 100mph ball and go all around the park hell-bent only on attaining the mark, to then see a young man bowl at 90mph with fantastic control of length and swing to both right and left-hander, put the 'Rawalpindi Rickshaw's' performance not only in the shade, but in the garage and up on bricks. Anderson, although understandably proud of those early performances, does look back with a degree of regret: "Looking back, I think I got a bit carried away with that side of my game."

I tell Anderson a story about a cricketer I played a lot of matches with. He was a swing bowler, not with the pace of Anderson, but an effective bowler on his day. But this player, more often than not sadly, showed a complete lack of instinct in recognising when the ball wasn't swinging for him.

"Everyone laughs, before Anderson unwinds from his paralysis and quips: 'I just can't multi-task…'"

> "After this season for Lancs I have matured and been able to recognise situations and react to them. It was pretty flat at Old Trafford last year and I had to be more patient."

He would put any lack of movement in the air down to the release of the ball not being quite right, or him bowling the ball a little too short, or without the right velocity. As much as anyone would tell him that it was simply a day where the ball just wasn't swinging and that he should pull his length back so the batsman had to work harder for his runs, that very next ball, in this bowler's mind, it might be the one that swung late and found the edge… 'BOOM!' Another delivery whistles through mid-off or midwicket for four.

Anderson reacts to the anecdote positively, seeing similarities: "That was me. But after this season for Lancs I have matured and been able to recognise situations and react to them. It was pretty flat at Old Trafford last year and I had to be more patient. I ended up bowling in excess of 500 overs for my wickets and I took them steadily without producing that one spell in the season where I took four wickets in eight overs and end up with six or seven wickets in the innings. I only managed one five-fer."

And to take his wickets steadily is no bad thing for a bowler like James Anderson. He played all season in a Lancashire side that ended up winning the second division, in a bowling attack that included stalwarts Glen Chapple and Dominic Cork, bolstered by overseas players Muttiah Muralitharan, Andrew Symonds and Murali Kartik, with further back-up from Gary Keedy, Sajid Mahmoond, Kyle Hogg and Tom Smith. Being the county's top wicket-taker with 60 victims, was another advance for the bowler.

As a person, Anderson seems more 'humble beginnings' than 'England pin-up'. For someone who has had his fair share of photographs taken, it doesn't look something he is supremely comfortable doing. At one stage he's directed by the photographer to adapt his pose in a certain way, just as I ask him another question – the complication throws Anderson who sits rigid and is unable to speak. Everyone laughs, before Anderson unwinds from his paralysis and quips: "I just can't multi-task…"

But according to John Abrahams, team manager of England under 19s and former Lancashire captain, Anderson is no softie: "He is from a lovely family, but there is definitely a bit of spite in him. You should see him on the football field – he doesn't like to lose. He's massively competitive."

In looking at what elements make the perfect paceman, one attribute was missing from the bowling profile – the ability to swing the cricket ball. There are few people in cricket who can maintain their pace when pitching the ball up to the bat. Many bowlers have been able to lever the ball in short at pace, but few, Pakistan's Waqar Younis being a notable exception, can bowl the ball from a decent height and hustle the batsman on the front foot. Fewer still can swing the ball at 88-90mph as Anderson can. He has the priceless knack of being able to get good players out.

We finish the interview oddly. Shaking hands in front of a giant image of Anderson, pictured as part of a cricketing montage up on one of the walls inside the academy building. It was taken when Anderson was flying high, taking hat-tricks and wickets for fun. With Glamorgan's Simon Jones not on the initial leg of the winter tour programme the chance is there for Anderson to re-establish himself as a top-flight performer and one of cricket's poster boys once again. The skills are in place, the hard work has been undertaken and with the hair returned 'au naturel', bad luck shouldn't be an issue. If only he could hire the injured Welshman's shoulders for a few months… ●

Stephen Fry's Greatest Ever XI

Actor, presenter, writer and broadcaster Stephen Fry loves his cricket. He let All Out Cricket's Monisha Rajesh into the secret of his favourite team of all time.

I We'll open with The Master: Jack Hobbs. In a thirty-year career, which saw him playing from the Golden Age of Edwardian cricket right through to the mid-thirties, he amassed 197 centuries and scored over 61,000 first class runs. They say he saw the ball earlier than any of his contemporaries and relished all conditions from dry to sticky-as-hell. They also report that he was a truly great cover field. A professional who was a true gentleman, he was knighted in 1953.

II Hobbs's most famous opening partnership was with Herbert Sutcliffe, but I am going to send him in with Sunil Gavaskar, the Indian run machine who scored 10,000 runs at an average of over 50.

III That's the easy part, the openers. Who should come in at number three? Well that's even more of a no-brainer. The entire world team would obviously have to be built around the man you could confidently call the greatest cricketer who ever lived: I've never heard of another sportsman who dominated his game as completely as the Don dominated cricket. He averaged, as every schoolboy knows, 99.94 and demolished all the bowlers of his day, scoring at a furious rate and with the twinkliest footwork imaginable. Like Gavaskar, a short man, he saw the ball so early that (judging from the film of the day) he appeared to be able to go back, forward, back and then forward again to a fast delivery.

IIII Two more short men are vying for number four: Sachin Tendulkar and Brian Lara. Lara's average of 53 is not as high as Tendulkar's 57 and I'm also inclined to trust the little wizard in tougher conditions. Lara is more than just a flat track bully, but I do believe that Sachin earns his place. I'll never forget my first sight of him when, aged 17, he came to England and outplayed men nearly twice his age.

V At five, who else but Sir Viv? The great Antiguan batsman could demolish any bowler in the world with speed and style.

VI At six I'd put Ian Botham: the great hero of my generation, he may not have been as aesthetically pleasing as any of the others, but he could turn a match with bat and ball like no one else. An amazingly athletic fielder too.

VII At seven, the greatest all-rounder of them all, Sir Garfield Sobers: as we know, he once hit six sixes in an over. His bowling was matchless in his day: fast over the wicket left-hander and back of the hand slow unorthodox too. One of the best leg-side fielders you could hope to see.

VIII At eight, a wicketkeeper and no keeper could furnish you with more runs than the terrifying Adam Gilchrist. I don't of course want him to be anything close to his destructive best against England, ever, or we'll definitely be in trouble. What's the point of bowling out six batsman if this monster then comes to the crease and hits a rapid eighty?

IX At nine, the greatest spinner there ever was, the man who transformed the game with his ripping leg breaks, his wicked top-spinners and his devastating googlies. The bleached bad boy, Shane Warne.

X/XI We'll bring up the tail with two of the fastest and meanest pacemen in history, Glenn McGrath and Dennis Lillee. GM bowls as straight as any man I've ever seen and, like Lillee, has got smarter and better with age.

Where are Rhodes and Barnes and Chappell and Imran and Kapil Dev and Hutton and Hammond and Boycott and Barrington and all the others? Where indeed: insane to leave them out of any team, but you only wanted eleven. AOC

THE FIRST TOUR

Has it really been 12 years since the first Barmy Army tour? It still only seems like yesterday to me. I was a young whippersnapper of 23 then and was loving being involved in every match, party and celebration that a tour had to offer. By Ian Golden

By the way, did I forget to mention that at that time England were crap. None of this Ashes winning lark for us. We lost the first two tests and were held to a draw in the third. Every run was a celebration, every century was a victory, all we had was our sense of humour – something the Aussies were seriously lacking. One of our jokes was printed on a T-shirt – "We came here with our backpacks, you with ball and chains." It wasn't officially the first Barmy Army T-shirt but came be treated as such now.

Then came Adelaide. At that time, the Adelaide test was traditionally the fourth such encounter, one that happened after the World Series, and I'm not talking baseball here. Ah, the world has changed so much since then, cricket especially.

But I digress. Yes, England were crap. We had a witty ditty at the time…

"We never win at home and we never win away, We lost last week and we'll lose today, We don't give a f*** cos we're all p***ed up. England Cricket Club, OK!"

That summed up the tour of 1994-95… apart from Adelaide. We went into the fifth day and we were 20-1 to actually win the match. The General put $100 on us to win for that price if I remember rightly and he ended up buying drinks that night. For those who haven't quite got the script yet, yes we won the match. "Daffy's supposed to mean duck, not ten runs an over" said the disgruntled Channel Ten news announcer that night after Phil deFreitas was the hero. I also remember Phil Tufnell making a great catch in the day, then getting wrecked in the night and leading the pub in a chorus of "If you've all f***ed an Aussie clap your hands." And before you think about suing Phil, I've got the video to prove it!

"We never win at home and we never win away,
We lost last week and we'll lose today,
We don't give a f*** cos we're all p***ed up.
England Cricket Club, OK!"

Yes we did go mad about that win. In the fifth test in Perth, we were selling T-shirts saying "Victory in Adelaide, I was there". I remember one Aussie commenting to me, "One win and you lot go mad". Well, yes we did and why shouldn't we?

However Adelaide 95 was memorable for more than just that win, it was the city where the Barmy Army officially or unofficially (I'm not sure which) launched. I'm proud to say that I was part of that launch. About 20 or 30 of us had T-shirts printed up and even had our names monogrammed on them. I was "Ian the Taff". We had "Chopper", "The General", "Leafy", "McGiff", "Monty", "Yorkshire Gav"

and many other memorable names from the past. We were "Atherton's Barmy Army" then, we had to change our name for the summer of 1995 because Michael didn't want his name associated with us… just in case!

It was thanks to the Australian press that we were nicknamed the Barmy Army. We started singing "Atherton's Barmy Army" in Melbourne and they picked up on that. It's just an old football song but the press thought we were a bit nuts to travel all round the country and be happy all the time even when we lose. For the Aussies, winning is everything – think Shane Warne. For us, think Tufnell – happy days.

Of course everyone else wanted

ENGLAND'S BARMY ARMY

The General
leading his troops
↓

"I remember one Aussie commenting to me, 'One win and you lot go mad'"

T-shirts, caps, stubbie holders, shorts and an organisation was born. Even the Aussies wanted to be part of it. They loved us out there – TV interviews, radio slots, newspaper articles, autographs, women. They even had a yellow T-shirt of their own "Taylor's Barmy Army – 3-1 – not bad for a bunch of convicts". Shame that wasn't kept up, we could have had a whole new market to sell to.

England lost the test series 3-1 and we partied all night in Perth following the final day of the tour. We'd hired a night club for this do. All blokes needed tickets to get in but for women it was free. The TV companies

also caught wind of it and turned up to film the frolics. Like I said – they loved us out there. The players turned up of course - they always came to our parties back then.

Both Yorkshire Gav and I pulled Aussie birds that night. While my fling lasted a mere couple of weeks, I believe Gav actually married his, had kids, got divorced, moved to Coogee and opened up a bricklaying business – not all necessary in that order.

Yes, there was nothing more memorable than Australia 94-95. After all, that's where the Barmy Army started and long may it continue.

IN MY DAY

Things were different 'back then', whatever job you're in. We caught up with a handful of county players to ask what it was like for them, making their debuts a few (and some a few more than a few) years ago.

DOUGIE BROWN
Warwickshire, 1991/94

AOC: What do you remember about your debut way back in 1991?

DB: Well, the start was a bit different to how I'd always envisaged it.

AOC: How do you mean?

DB: I walked into the first-team dressing room to be greeted by: "What the ***k are you doing here?" "Err...I've been called into the firsts," I replied, a bit sheepishly. "Well, turn round, go outside and start again by knocking!" And so I did.

AOC: How did you get on in the game after such a friendly welcome?

DB: Hmmm, I picked up Azharuddin's wicket. LBW shuffling across his stumps, if I remember rightly. And we won. But that was only my one-day debut. I had to wait another three years for my Championship call-up. That was against Surrey and we were struggling when I came to the crease at number ten. Made a fifty, put on a hundred, won the game, won the Championship. Wish every game could be a debut!

> I walked into the first-team dressing room to be greeted by: "What the ***k are you doing here?"

NADEEM SHAHID
Essex, 1989

AOC: What was it like in the Chelmsford dressing room before your debut?

NS: I was nervous, visibly quaking with fear. I had no idea what to expect.

AOC: And, how was it?

NS: Well, initially I thought that I'd been employed as a batsman, but I didn't face a ball the entire game. Originally I was in at six, but I was demoted to eight as we looked for quick runs. We declared at two down in the first innings and only lost four in the second so my only contribution was bowling a few overs against an in-form Chris Lewis. It wasn't so bad in the end, though as my first over in first-class cricket was a maiden and I took wickets in both innings.

MICHAEL POWELL
Glamorgan, 1997

MP: I made my debut in 1997 against Oxford University and scored 200 not out.

AOC: Yeah, yeah but what about against a real team?

MP: OK, my debut for the first team was against Worcester at New Road the same year.

AOC: And?

MP: 0. Stumped Bumpy Rhodes down the leg-side off Gavin Haynes. Felt a right idiot. Medium-pacer as well. Just stupid. And embarrassing. And I didn't get too many second dig either. From the penthouse to the sh…, doghouse I guess.

AOC: So what do you remember most?

MP: Just playing with brilliant, brilliant players like Waqar, Steve Watkin, Matt Maynard, Steve James, Hugh Morris. It was the year we won the Championship and I'd really had very little to do with the guys before that, just working away in the seconds. I wasn't that nervous because to be honest, growing up I didn't really think I'd play cricket for a living – didn't really want to even – so I never had that overwhelming desire to play my first game and I was fairly relaxed about it. It was great to play at New Road though. There are some pretty ropy grounds around so looking back, to kick off at the Parks then go to New Road was a bit special.

DAVID LEATHERDALE
Worcestershire, 1988

AOC: Congratulations on your retirement. Can you remember back to your debut, though?

DL: Yes, I think so. Just. It was against Leicestershire at Grace Road. I'd been playing for the 2s at Lancaster the day before and was called up because someone was injured.

AOC: What was your first thought when you got the call?

DL: Not sure if I can repeat that here but it went along the lines of 'Oh dear me'.

AOC: So you were nervous then?

DL: I'm not sure which was worse, walking into our first team dressing room with the likes of Ian Botham, Graham Dilley, Neale Radford, Steve Rhodes, Phil Neale, Richard Illingworth or walking out to face Jon Agnew, Winston Benjamin, Les Taylor and George Ferris. I was very much the minnow amongst these top calibre players. To make things worse I got hit on the head, third ball, by Les Taylor. An eye-opener to say the least.

> To make things worse I got hit on the head, third ball, by Les Taylor. An eye-opener to say the least.

JON LEWIS
Essex, 1990

AOC: Do you remember all the details of your debut?

JL: It was for Essex in 1990. Against Surrey at the Oval. Last Championship game of the season. Is this the kind of thing you're after?

AOC: Perfect. How about from a personal point of view?

JL: I was with the team as 12th man but Mark Waugh got sick the night before so I was drafted in. I wasn't nervous as I'd travelled as 12th man before, doing the junior dogsbody stuff like running bets on horses for Waugh, but I knew that it was pure luck that had got me this far. The coach, Keith Fletcher, kept trying to build it up, telling me that I was there on my merit, but I wasn't fooled.

AOC: Well he obviously said something right as you scored a century in that match.

JL: It was a flat pitch and Waqar wasn't on good form, so once again I got lucky. You could tell he didn't really want to bowl; he was still a bit injured. He only bowled two spells on the first day and none after that. We actually travelled home together on the tube after day one and he was telling me about his injuries and that he was concerned about playing for Pakistan the following week! My advice to him was not to bother about this little game and concentrate on being fit for his country. I was honestly concerned about him, but I guess it worked in my favour as well.

AOC: Hmmmm….

"I wasn't nervous as I'd travelled as 12th man before, doing the junior dogsbody stuff like running bets on horses for Waugh."

GLEN CHAPPLE
Lancashire, 1992

AOC: So, were you nervous?

GC: Didn't really have time to get nervous. I was playing for the seconds the day before and we were at Crosby near Liverpool. I was fielding on the boundary when the manager came round to tell me that I was playing with the firsts the next day in Brighton. He then had to go back to my house to pick up some extra gear. I remember thinking that I didn't want him to go round 'cos the house was a state as my parents were away and I'd had a few mates round. That was worse than the game itself!

AOC: Were you not excited about getting your big break?

GC: We had so many injuries and illnesses in the first team at the time, so most of us were newbies. I'd travelled down with Ronnie Irani and there were a couple more of us when we arrived. It was just like a slightly more important second eleven game. There were some big names in the opposition – David Smith, Ian Salisbury, Tony Pigott – but we just got on and did what we had to do. It was a nice, flat pitch, I bowled ok, didn't get a wicket, and got 20 not out. Nothing exciting, but nothing to put me off either.

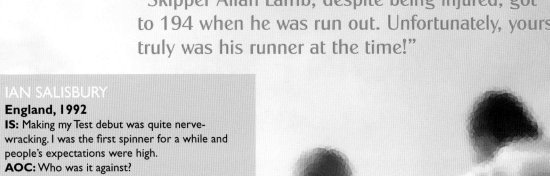

"Skipper Allan Lamb, despite being injured, got to 194 when he was run out. Unfortunately, yours truly was his runner at the time!"

IAN SALISBURY
England, 1992

IS: Making my Test debut was quite nerve-wracking. I was the first spinner for a while and people's expectations were high.

AOC: Who was it against?

IS: Pakistan at Lord's. Waqar Younis was bowling pretty quick but it was Mushtaq Ahmed that got me, hit wicket, for four. That was a bit embarrassing on debut, but it's never happened again thankfully. I took five wickets in the match, the first being Javed Miandad, caught by Beefy. Unfortunately it pretty much went downhill from there.

RICHARD MONTGOMERIE
Northamptonshire, 1991

AOC: Do you remember what year you made your Championship debut?

RM: 1992, perhaps? It was for Northamptonshire against Surrey.

AOC: Do you remember getting the call?

RM: I was still at university and wasn't expecting to play for the firsts at all that year so getting the call was very exciting. By the time it came to the actual game I was really nervous, especially at the thought of facing Waqar Younis!

AOC: So how did things pan out?

RM: Waqar was injured so that was good! I only managed two and seven, which wasn't ideal but skipper Allan Lamb, despite being injured, got to 194 when he was run out. Unfortunately, yours truly was his runner at the time! Not sure how well that went down, but I didn't play again for another two years.....

HARMONY HISTORIES
ASHES 98/99 ONWARDS

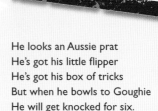

PART THREE

BC: You were saying that the Ashes Tour of 98/99 was understandably far more organised.

Leafy: Gary Taylor produced the first Songs of Praise booklet - basically a two page sheet with lyrics on it. Essentially, the fun ditties from the 94/5 tour were replaced with some longer versions. The 94/5 tour was spontaneous, the 98/9 songs had planning hence the longer versions, but still with a lot of spontaneity.

The Aussies love the English, you might find it quite strange
'Cos we sent them all down under, with only balls and chains
And when they see the English, they always shout and scream
But when they had the chance to vote they voted for the Queen!
God save your gracious Queen
Long live your noble Queen
God save your Queen (you're a convict)
Send her victorious
Happy and glorious
Long to reign over you
God save your Queen.
(Courtesy of Gary Taylor)

BC: Shane Warne presumably had his own song?

Leafy: Yes. To the tune of "My Old Man's A Dustman"... Which is always the most popular adaptation.

Shane Warne is an Aussie
He wears a baggy cap
He's got a Nike earring

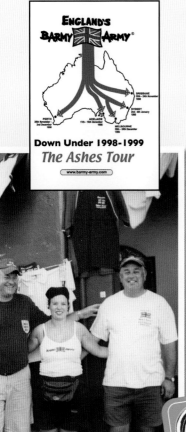

He looks an Aussie prat
He's got his little flipper
He's got his box of tricks
But when he bowls to Goughie
He will get knocked for six.

BC: What was the Mark Waugh story?

Leafy: That was a good example of a more spontaneous type of song, reacting to events. Without raking it up - there was allegedly a scandal involving bookies and what have you. So the Mark Waugh song reflected that. Listen – all we are doing in this book is recording honestly what was sung. But – as with all Barmy chants – it's a bit of a laugh. No one takes it seriously.

BC: And in no way does it reflect the views of the Barmy Army or Barmy Army Productions, your Honour.

'Mark Waugh is an Aussie
He wears a Baggy Cap
And when he saw the bookies cash
He said I'm having that

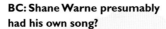

> "Jerusalem seemed logical and the most powerful song to inspire the players, since then we have made every effort to get people to sing it, and it's worked."

He shared it out with Warnie
They went and had some beers
And when the ACB found out
They covered it up for years'

BC: Tell me about "Jerusalem". I know that this has always been important to you.

Leafy: Yes, me and lots of Barmies have always felt that the Barmy Army ought to have an anthem as well as God Save Our Queen. Jerusalem seemed logical and the most powerful song to inspire the players, since then we have made every effort to get people to sing it, and it's worked. So much so that now NPower actively get behind the song, particularly during the Ashes in 2005; because of this they were put up for an award for innovation at the Hollis Sponsorship Awards later that summer.

And did those feet in ancient time
Walk upon England's mountain green?
And was the holy Lamb of God
On England's pleasant pastures seen?
And did the countenance divine
Shine forth upon our clouded hills?
And was Jerusalem builded here
Among those dark satanic mills?
Bring me my bow of burning gold!
Bring me my arrows of desire!
Bring me my spear! O clouds, unfold!
Bring me my chariot of fire!
I will not cease from mental fight,
Nor shall my sword sleep in my hand,
Till we have built Jerusalem
In England's green and pleasant land.

Another song which reflects the sprit of that tour....

(To the tune of Yellow Submarine)
In the town where I was born, there

lived a man who was a thief
And he told me of his life, stealing bread and sh*gging sheep.
So they put him in the nick, and then a magistrate he went to see
He said "put him on a ship, to the convict colony"
You all live in a convict colony, a convict colony, a convict colony
You all live in a convict colony, a convict colony, a convict colony
2,3,4
(Courtesy of the Grim Reaper)

BC: Did people still sing Ball and Chain from the 94 tour?

Leafy: Yes, but with a difference. We tagged on The House of the Rising Sun at the front so that the song came as a bit of a surprise. Not after the first time we sang it of course but it went down well.....

Beefy is presented with funds raised during the tour for Lukemia research

Slazenger persuade us to sacrifice one of our members at Lords by inflating this 9ft costume as Hicky walked out to bat with a blue bat – it never happened and Andy was ejected and enjoyed the rest of the match in the Lords Tavern

There is a house in New Orleans, They call the Rising Sun
It's been the ruin of many a poor boy, oh Lord I know I'm one
One foot on the platform, one foot on the train
I'm going back to New Orleans, to wear my ball and chain
1,2,
BALL AND CHAIN! BALL AND CHAIN!
WE CAME HERE WITH BACKPACKS

YOU WITH BALL AND CHAIN
BALL AND CHAIN! BALL AND CHAIN!
WE CAME HERE WITH BACKPACKS
YOU WITH BALL AND CHAIN!
(Courtesy of Andy Evans)

The end of the tour song was particularly catchy I remember:
'We've been to Adelaide
We've been Tasmania
We've been to Perth
We've been to Brisbane too
We've been the MCG
We've been the SCG
And all because cos England we love you'

BC: Can you remember any Aussie songs from the tour?
Leafy: Yes, the same 3 from the 94/5 tour.

BC: We're now up to the World Cup 99 in England. The Barmy Army are pretty well organised by this point. How did this manifest itself?
Leafy: In lots of different ways. A "Come on England" Barmy Army single was released. Barmy Army - in conjunction with Telstar Records who produced the football hit "Vindaloo" teamed together to produce the CD to get behind the England Team for their World Cup campaign.

The Barmy Video for the song was filmed on Kew Green with stars like Roni Irani, Ian Botham, Dickie Bird, Robin Smith, Mark Butcher, Chris Tarrant, Alex Tudor and Faye from Steps.

Cheque is handed over raised by the Army for street cricket in JNB

BC What happened?
Leafy: Unfortunately we were knocked out at the start of the Super 6s just as the song was released, so Telstar knocked it on the head.

BC: So that was the end of it?
Leafy: No, in fact we got the CD back off Telstar and used it as a give-away. It drove lots of parents mad because the kids kept singing it. Despite everything it still got to number 42. It did provide inspiration for the BA Colts section however so it wasn't all negative.

BC: And there was a Barmy Army pop promo. Fame?
Leafy: Ronni Irani was in it and Fay from Steps. Great fun.

ENGLAND'S BARMY ARMY®

1999 - 2000

1ST TEST	25 - 29 NOVEMBER	JOHANNESBURG
2ND TEST	9 - 13 DECEMBER	PORT ELIZABETH
3RD TEST	26 - 30 DECEMBER	DURBAN
4TH TEST	2 - 6 JANUARY	CAPE TOWN
5TH TEST	14 - 18 JANUARY	CENTURION

www.barmy-army.com

BC: Moving on to South Africa 99/00. Any songs that stand out?
Leafy: Well the song which I personally think is the best invented by the Barmy Army and one which has been acknowledged by the victim as good fun is the Alan Donald song. Now this was a reinvention of a frankly pretty forthright song which was sung on a previous tour and was adapted for the better on the back of the World Cup incident when Klusener called for a run and Alan froze. Apparently, this continued to be sung to him in the nets by his team mates and, according to him, is still sung to him now....

(To the tune of Da Doo Ron Ron)
'My name is Alan Donald and I
should've run
Run run Alan, Run Run Run
Zulu called a single but I stood still
Run run Alan, Run Run Run
Wooh, I had a panic attack
Wooh, and I dropped my Bat
Wooh, I should've run
Run run Alan, Run Run Run'

BODDINGTONS BARMY ARMY
SONG SHEET

Away in a Mnager
Awat in a manger
No room for a bed
The little Lord Jesus
Lay down and he said
EN'GER'LAND
EN'GER'LAND
EN'GER'LAND

The Barmy Boys
I-OH-I-OH
We are the Barmy Boys
I-OH-I-OH
We are the Barmy Boys
We're England's famous cricket fans
Who travel near adn far
If we're not singing
You'll find us at the bar!

Cheer Up
(to the tune of "Day Dream
Believer")
Cheer up Bob Willis
Oh what can it mean
To the worst cricket pundit
On the Sky commentary team

Goughie
E-I-E-I-E-I-O
Off to Cape Town we must go
When we win the series
This is what we'll sing
We are England
We are England
Goughie is our King

Here for the Cricket
(to be sung to anyone singing football
songs)
Here for the cricket
We're only here for the cricket
Here for the cricket
We're only here for the cricket

Hansie Cronje
(to the tune of "Dad's Army")
Who do you think you are kidding
Hansie Cronje
If you think old England's done
We are the boys who will stop your
little game
We are the boys who will make you
think again
So who do you think you are kidding
Hansie Cronje
If you think old England's done!

JONTY (or any South African)
One man went to bed
Went to bed with Jonty
One man and his sheep BAAAA
Went to bed with Jonty

Two men went to bed...
etc., up to eleven (stand on eleven)

SRI LANKA 2001

22-26 Feb	1st Test	Galle
7-11 Mar	2nd Test	Kandy
15-19 Mar	3rd Test	Colombo
23 March	1st One Day	Dambulla
25 March	2nd One Day	Colombo
27 March	3rd One Day	Colombo

www.barmy-army.com

Colombo 2001 the noise carried out to the middle

17 03 '01

You can make a racket out the but the locals compete well.

Sri Lanka 2003

Nov 18 - 1st ODI, Dambulla.	Dec 2-6 - 1st Test, Galle.
Nov 21 - 2nd ODI, Colombo (RPS).	Dec 10-14 - 2nd Test, Kandy
Nov 23 - 3rd ODI, Colombo (RPS).	Dec 18-22 - 3rd Test, Colombo (SSC)

www.barmy-army.com

BC: Sri Lanka 01?

Leafy: Its interesting over there, the attitude towards the singing. Now as we know, Murali will never tour Australia again due to the abuse he gets over there, but whenever he hears the Barmy songs he always smiles. Maybe he doesn't quite understand what we are getting at or maybe he's just a good sport. I think he doesn't mind it personally.

'Throw throw throw the ball
Gently through the air
Murali, Murali, Murali, Murali
Where is Daryl Hair?
NO Ball'
Chuck, chuck, chuck the ball
Gently down the seam
Murali, Murali, Murali, Murali
Chucks it like a dream'

Lion Beer song:
'In the jungle, the Kandy jungle
There's Lion Beer tonight

In the jungle,
the Kandy jungle
There's Lion Beer tonight
A win away, A win awaySSS..'

When this bl**dy Tour is over
When this bl**dy tour is over
Oh how happy I will be
On the plane back home to England
No more hot curries for me
No more cheating Aussie Umpires
No more catches off the grass
We will tell these Tuk Tuk drivers
To stick their rupees up their ****'

Justin Langer went into one in his Press Conference… He accused the English fans of not knowing what they talked about and just being fat drunks basically.

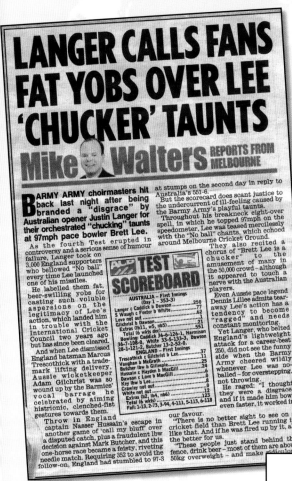

LANGER CALLS FANS FAT YOBS OVER LEE 'CHUCKER' TAUNTS

Mike Walters REPORTS FROM MELBOURNE

BARMY ARMY choirmasters hit back last night after being branded a "disgrace" by Australian opener Justin Langer for their orchestrated "chucking" taunts at 97mph pace bowler Brett Lee.

As the fourth Test erupted in controversy and a serious sense of humour failure, Langer took on 3,000 England supporters who bellowed "No ball" every time Lee launched one of his missiles.

He labelled them fat, beer-swilling yobs for casting such voluble aspersions on the legitimacy of Lee's action, which landed him in trouble with the International Cricket Council two years ago but has since been cleared.

And when Lee dismissed England batsman Marcus Trescothick with a trademark lifting delivery, Aussie wicketkeeper Adam Gilchrist was so wound up by the Barmies' vocal barrage he celebrated by aiming histrionic, clenched-fist gestures towards them.

Throw in England captain Nasser Hussain's escape in another game of 'call my bluff' over a disputed catch, plus a fraudulent lbw decision against Mark Butcher, and this one-horse race became a feisty, riveting needle match. Requiring 352 to avoid the follow-on, England had stumbled to 97-3

at stumps on the second day in reply to Australia's 551-6.

But the scorecard does scant justice to the undercurrent of ill-feeling caused by the Barny Army's playful taunts.

Throughout his breakneck eight-over spell, in which he topped 97mph on the speedometer, Lee was teased mercilessly with the "No ball" chants, which echoed around the Melbourne Cricket Ground.

They also recited a chorus of "Brett Lee is a chucker" to the amusement of many in the 50,000 crowd - although it appeared to touch a nerve with the Australian players.

Even Aussie pace legend Dennis Lillee admits tear-away Lee's action has a tendency to become "ragged" and needs constant monitoring.

Yet Langer, who belted England's lightweight attack for a career-best 250, did not see the funny side when the Barmy Army cheered wildly whenever Lee was no-balled - for overstepping, not throwing.

He raged: "I thought they were a disgrace, and if it made him bowl even faster, it worked in our favour.

"There is no better sight to see on a cricket field than Brett Lee running in like that. And if he was fired up by it, all the better for us.

"These people just stand behind the fence, drink beer - most of them are about 50kg overweight - and make ridiculous

TEST SCOREBOARD

AUSTRALIA – First Innings
(Day 1 - 353-3)

Langer c Caddick b Dawson	250
S Waugh c Foster b White	77
Love not out	21
Gilchrist b Dawson	2
Extras (lb11, w5, nb5)	51
Total (6 wkts dec)	551
Bowling: Caddick 36-6-126-1, Harmison 36-7-108-0, White 33-5-133-3, Dawson 28-1-121-2, Butcher 13-2-52-0.	

ENGLAND – First Innings

Trescothick c Gilchrist b Lee	37
Vaughan b McGrath	11
Butcher lbw b Gillespie	24
Hussain c Hayden b MacGill	6
Dawson c Love b MacGill	8
Key lbw b Lee	0
Crawley not out	0
White not out	0
Extras (b2, lb4, nb6)	123
Total (6 wkts)	
Fall-1-13, 2-73, 3-94, 4-111, 5-113, 6-118	

BC: Back to New Zealand 02.

Leafy: My favourite moment from New Zealand was the Test when Thorpey got a double century - being dropped by Nathan Astle in the process. Astle then proceed to score a double century himself in incredibly quick time, As he walked off feeling pretty pleased with himself one solitary

Farmy Army singer stood up and to the tune of OOh My Darling Clementine¹ sang:

'Nathan Astle, Nathan Astle
You should've won the match
Even though you scored 200
You dropped the vital catch'

Astle just shook his head, as if to say - you can't win. This chant was then taken up immediately by the rest of the Farmies & Barmies. This was a great spontaneous moment.

Other pro England songs include:
Now Hoggies the King of the Swingers
An England VIP
He has a bowl
The wickets roll
The Aussies out by tea

Oh, oo oo oo
I wanna bowl like you oo oo
Not bat like you
Bowl like you
Oh oo oo oo

Oh yes its true oo oo
I wanna bowl like you oo oo
Not bat like you
Bowl like you
Oh oo oo oo

BC: The Ashes 02/03?

Leafy: Business as usual really, still only 3 songs from the Aussies and lots more invention from the Barmies. The highlight of the tour was the no-balling of Brett Lee and the comments from Justin Langer in the press conference afterwards.

BC: Please expand

Leafy: We were giving Brett Lee some understandable stick about No Balling – similar to the way the Aussies do to Murali – and Justin Langer went into one in his Press Conference in the process of trying to defend Brett. He accused the English fans of not knowing what they talked about and just being fat drunks basically.

BC: Harsh but fair?

Leafy: No comment.

Anyway, the next day the Barmy Army arrived with lots of new songs and gags to give to the Australian supporters and fielders alike. The atmosphere was brilliant all day, and although we lost we did get 5 of their wickets cheaply and regained some momentum both on the pitch and off. So thanks to Justin Langer for that as we moved on to Sydney and a famous vistory.

The songs got more and more complex by this stage and we

Barmy Army support the English Girls Hockey Team.

The first Barmy Army Cadet! ➜

regularly received long penned versions of songs through our email at barmyarmy.com. We continue to get these to this day.

Some examples:

WONDERWALL..
Today is gonna be the day that we're gonna sing a song for you.
By now you should've somehow realised that's what we're here to do.
And I don't believe that anybody sings as bad as you.

Aussie Convicts
Backbeat, the word is on the street that you can't even write a song
I'm sure, you've heard it all before, but c'mon Aussies prove us wrong
'Cos I don't believe that anybody's quite as thick as you

Aussie Convicts
The "oh aah" song you sing for Glenn is so sad
And "Warney Warney Warney" is just as bad
There are many songs that I would like to hear from you

But you don't know how, (don't know how)
'Cos maybe, (maybe) you'll never find a song to play me, (play me)
'Cos after all, YOU CAN SING SOD ALL!
(Courtesy of Leafy & Dermot Reeve)

12 Days of Christmas
On the 12th Day of Christmas My Nasser Sent to me.
12 weeks of drinking
11 Fit players
10 Aussie wickets
9 short for Warnie
8 all the pies

7 saucy Sheila's
6 Brett Lee Chuckers
5 Haemorrhoids
'Ouch'
4 more runs
3 proud lions
2 Cheating Umpires
And a win at the SCG
(Thanks to the Balcony Boys especially Scunny)

The Sydney Test on this tour was the last and we were 4-0 down. However the last 2 days of the Test saw the Barmy Army fill the ground, with Day 5 being nearly all British fans. The atmosphere

was amazing and the singing was unbelievably loud. Unfortunately we did such a good job, that for the 2006/7 series Cricket Australia have decided to split the Barmy Army up – can't really blame them I suppose.

BC: The next two tours - South Africa and the West Indies?
Leafy: these were 2 great tours, where England were very successful. A new brand of Barmy Army fan supported each Test match, even the loss at Cape Town,

supporting the team as loudly now that they were winning regularly. Both tours were massive triumphs and have been the most successful off the pitch in Barmy Army History. The Sean Pollock Cricket World Cup song came out of this…

BC: Based on what?
Leafy: The song tells the story. Pollock miscounted during the World Cup and South Africa were knocked out.

(to the tune of Da Doo Ron Ron)
My name is Sean Pollock and I cannot Count
One more run run, one more run run
I miscalculated and we got knocked out
One more run run, one more run run

Wooh we had a panic attack
Wooh and then I got the sack

One more run run, one more run run

Legend has it that Allan Donald was relieved that the song had moved on. He reminded Sean Pollock about singing the Allan Donald song to him at net practice. What goes around comes around!

BC: This brings us on to the Ashes 05. For the first time, the Barmy Army had managed to secure blocks of 150 tickets at each day of each test (apart from Lords). From the 2nd Test at Edgbaston the singing from the Army and the vocality of most of the crowds definitely had a helping hand with the result of the series. The red carpet was not laid out in its normal fashion for the Aussies; even at Lords the crowd tried their best to give the

← Aussie Tim Knight with Katie. They both made a big difference to how the Barmy is today!

Show me the way to Shane Warne's Villa, He's got his diet pills under his pillow, A dodgy bookie from Manila, And a Nurse on his mobile phone

↑ Barmy Army male voice choir – some of our best, or worst, singers sing to Gilo, Freddie and Vaughnie at Gilo's benefit dinner – a total honour

Aussies a hard time.
Leafy: Obviously the best series ever. Great singing, tension, everything, and - in the end - a great result.

BC: Favourite song?
Leafy: All of them – but I liked Gaz's song from last summer. As I've said – we know that Warney doesn't take himself too seriously and has always taken our songs in the right spirit – it's a bit of fun.

BC: A joke?
Leafy: That's right.

Shane Warne's Villa (Amarillo)
As the day is dawning
On sunny Kennington morning
we're on the brink of history
And I can hear that Ashes Urn calling

I hear her calling out to me, Whooah
We're on the verge of victory, Whooah
but before she comes to me
There's somewhere I must go---oh!

Show me the way to Shane Warne's Villa
He's got his diet pills under his pillow
A dodgy bookie from Manila
And a Nurse on his mobile phone

LA-LA LAR LAR LAR LAR LAR LAR..
FAT G*T!
LA-LA LAR LAR LAR LAR LAR LAR..

TAKES A BUNG!
LA-LA LAR LAR LAR LAR LAR
LAR.. WARNEY'S ON HIS MOBILE PHONE!

Now Down Unders calling
From the West to the East we're touring
Following Gatting's legacy
We won't give it up, not easily

I hear her calling out to me, Whooah
"Back to Lords and the MCC!"
Whooah
Retain her, and then we'll see
There's one place left to go--oh

Show me the way to Shane Warne's Villa
He's got his diet pills under his pillow
A dodgy bookie from Manila
And a Nurse on his mobile phone

LA-LA LAR LAR LAR LAR LAR LAR..
FAT G*T!
LA-LA LAR LAR LAR LAR LAR LAR..
TAKES A BUNG!
LA-LA LAR LAR LAR LAR LAR LAR
LAR.. WARNEY'S ON HIS MOBILE PHONE!

BC: The next tour?
Leafy: The next tour was the ill fated series in Pakistan. Again the song I've chosen was just a bit of a laugh and...

BC: Let me guess. It does not reflect the opinions of Barmy Army Productions in any way...

'Lets twist again
Like Shahid Afridi
Lets twist again
Like he did last year
Do you remember when
He got banned for ch**ting?'
Lets twist again.
Twisting time is here.

We managed to draw in India with a great win in Mumbai. Plus, a very good Barmy Army presence on the continent. And a few new pro England songs appeared

1. To the tune of "You are my sunshine".
"We are the army
the barmy army
oh we are mental
and we are mad
we are the loyalist
cricket supporters
that the world has ever had!
Courtesy of Gary Fulton

2. Alastair Cook - sung to tune of "Give it up". KC & The Sunshine Band.
"You flew out to India

when your country needed ya
hundred on debut
what a find

nana nana nana na na na na Alastair Cook
Ally Cook
Ally Ally Cook
repeat"
(Gary Fulton)

3. Paul Collingwood - to 'When the boat comes in!'
"Who will take his wicket
spinners he will pick it
never take his wicket
when Collingwood comes in!

drink with the army
sing with the army
drink with the army
when Collingwood comes in

drink with army
drink with army
drink with army
drink with army
drink with army
when Collingwood comes in."
(Gary Fulton)

4. Sajid Mahmood - courtesy of Ricky Ward - to the tune of 'Blue

Moon'
"Mahmood his name is Sajid Mahmood his name is Sajid Mahmood his name is Sajid Mahmood "

BC: Paul, thanks mate. A pretty good summary of the Barmy Songbook to date. Do you have anything to add?
Leafy: Yes, I have probably only remembered half of the songs. Please just keep them coming in. We always need new material!

Mitsubishi Motors sponsor a 50ft Barmy Army banner, that not surprisingly wins the Toyota Banner Competition. It was subsequently stolen from the railings outside Trent Bridge CG during the England vs West Indies test match, summer '95. Any information on this miraculous theft please contact us directly.

The all-time XI

of cricketers whose names sound a bit rude!

In batting order:

1. Sourav Ganguly (c) (India 1995)

2. John Badcock (Hampshire 1906)

3. Craig Cumming (New Zealand 2005)

4. Peter Willey (England 1976-1986)

5. John Fagge (Kent 1840s)

6. Geoff Humpage (wk) (Warwickshire keeper 1974-90)

7. Kenneth Fiddling (Northants 1940s)

8. Carl Tuckett (Leeward Islands 1994-2004)

9. Fred Titmus (England 1955-75)

10. Fanie de Villiers (South Africa 1993-98)

11. Anil Kumble (India 1990)

12th man: Dave Cock (Essex keeper 1940s)

4